Nicky Testaforte's

Black Book

50 Original Dark Drama and Comedy Scenes For Actors

Volume 1

Published by
Testaforte Entertainment

First US Print Edition August 2015
First Kindle Edition August 2015

Testaforte, Nicky

Black Book

50 Original Dark Drama and Comedy Scenes for Actors - Volume 1

Summary: A variety of original Drama and Comedy scenes derived from Television and Feature Film screenplays written by Author and Screenwriter Nicky Testaforte.

Thank you for your interest in these original scenes derived from my TV and Feature Film scripts.

This edition includes:

- 50 Scenes from 18 scripts
- Each 1 to 19 minutes long
- For 1 to 7 Characters
- Ranging from 15 to 60 years old

I've laid them out just like the source screenplays, so that each actor's sides are clearly delineated, plus no hanging indents make them easy to read.

Please enjoy as I wish you a long, fulfilling, uninterrupted and financially rewarding career in this business of show.

All the best,

Nicky Testaforte
August 2015
New York City

Follow me at @nickytestaforte for updates on all things Testaforte Entertainment.

Table of Contents

The Source Scripts

The Driver – *Drama Short*

A limo driver in a modified Town Car picks up unsuspecting people bound for their final destination.

Exacting Retribution – *Revenge Thriller*

A young boy survives the murder of his family and the murder of his stepfather. He channels that anger into a successful revenge for hire business.

Justified Retribution – *Revenge Thriller*

A woman redeems herself through martial arts and building a successful law firm after she's sexually assaulted at a fraternity party. She then sets out exacting revenge on each of the men responsible.

The Benefactor – *Half Hour TV Drama*

A wealthy disabled business man and his taxi driver associate dispense cash and vacation packages to those they deem worthy.

Ozzie's Limo – *Half Hour TV Dramedy*

A reluctant LA actress comes back east to help her aging father run his limo business. She quickly learns to deal with the off the wall characters and daily situations that confront her.

Dante's Limo – *Half Hour TV Comedy*

A caustic limo dispatcher spends his days managing drivers who consistently find themselves in comedically undesirable situations

Fake Commercials

Comedic inserts dropped in before fixed commercial breaks

Selected Scenes

Title: "The Driver"

Source: "The Driver" *Short Screenplay*

Genre: Drama

Tone: Dark

Approx. Length: 2 Minutes

Character 1: The Driver - *Male, 40's*

Character 2: Drunk Party Girl - *Female, 20's*

Scene Description:
Part One: Back of a Limo
Part Two: Shipping Container

PARTY GIRL

W Union Square. And step on it...

Hey, this isn't the way to the hotel.

DRIVER

I know. I need to teach you something.

PARTY GIRL

Let me out of this friggin car or I'm calling 911.

.

DRIVER

Be my guest. But if you glance down at your phone you'll see that you just lost your signal. So sorry, no white knight coming to your rescue tonight.

And, save your energy, those doors only open from the outside and the windows are tinted. So, no one can see you and there's no way out.

INT. SHIPPING CONTAINER - NIGHT
From the girl's POV we see a bright light shining at her. The Driver is seen reading the paper in a chair and looks up when he hears the girl coming out of her stupor.

The Female's arms and legs are spread as she's tied to the ceiling and floor suspended off the ground.

DRIVER
Bout time you woke up.

PARTY GIRL
(screaming)
Who are you and what do you want.

DRIVER
I'm Barney Fife and this is your final resting place.

What do you think of the place?

PARTY GIRL
You know, my parents have money, they'll pay you. I'll do anything you want if you let me go.

DRIVER
Anything?

PARTY GIRL
You name it. Let me go and it's yours.

DRIVER
Anything?

PARTY GIRL
Yes, now let me down!

DRIVER
Wow, thanks for the offer, but I don't need anything.

PARTY GIRL
Why are you doing this?

DRIVER
Uh, mommy issues? No
Bad childhood...No
Hate women...No

How bout you were stupid enough to get in my
car....That's it!

PARTY GIRL
You're fucking sick.

DRIVER
Nah, had a cold last week, but I'm fine now. Well,
it's time for me to go. Enjoy the hang...

PARTY GIRL
(pleading)
Wait, wait don't leave me here...

Help!!...Please help me!
#

Title: "Street Scene"

Source: "Exacting Retribution" *Feature Script*

Genre: Drama

Tone: Dark

Approx. Length: 2 Minutes

Character 1: JD Kendall **-** *Male, 40's*

Character 2: Mildred Fenwick - *Female, 60's*

Scene Description:
1960's suburban street, scene of a home invasion and murder.

MILDRED FENWICK

Oh! Officer it's so tragic, the boy came running to my house. His clothes are all bloody. All he kept saying was they're gone, they're gone.

MIKE COLLINS

OK, I'll go over and take a look. Please go inside now. Is the boy still with you?

MILDRED FENWICK

He's inside with my husband. Oh that poor boy. What will happen to him?

MIKE COLLINS

After I check the house, I'll call children's services. Please go back inside and wait for me.

Five X-Ray Two Five be advised multiple homicide 93 Franklin Road. Location secured, need morgue truck and children's services forthwith at this location.

MILDRED FENWICK
Is it true officer, are they all gone?

MIKE COLLINS
Yes ma'am, I'm sorry.

MILDRED FENWICK
Oh my lord, do you have any idea who could have done this?

MIKE COLLINS
Too early to tell. Now if you don't mind, I need you to tell me exactly what you saw and heard.

MILDRED FENWICK
Well Officer, I heard a loud bang. I had the window open, my bedroom faces the street. I got up to see what it was, figured it was just a car backfiring. I looked out; saw nothing, so I went to get a drink of water in my bathroom. Then I heard men's voices and a car taking off very fast.

I went downstairs, opened the door, went out to my porch, and looked down the street. They must have turned off, because the street was empty.

MIKE COLLINS
And then what did you do?

MILDRED FENWICK
Well I came back in and went into the kitchen to warm some milk to help me sleep. I was stirring the milk for a while, when I heard someone running up the porch steps and banging on the front door.

I shut the stove off, went to see who was there and I tell you Officer, I was frightened when I saw my neighbor Louise's son standing there in tears with blood all over his night clothes.

MIKE COLLINS
OK Mrs. Fenwick. I may have more questions later but I need to see the boy now. Where is he?

MILDRED FENWICK
In the parlor with my husband. He's been sobbing, I feel so sorry for him.
#

Title: "Kitchen Scene"

Source: "Exacting Retribution" *Feature Script*

Genre: Drama

Tone: Light

Approx. Length: 4 Minutes

Character 1: Mike Collins - *Male, 40's*

Character 2: Emily Collins - *Female, 40's*

Character 3: Billy Collins - *Male, 15*

Character 4: JD Kendall - *Male, 15*

Scene Description:
Family kitchen in the 1960's.

MIKE COLLINS
Hey Em, do you know where the boys are?

EMILY COLLINS
Billy said he and JD were going around the block to play with the other kids.

The back door flies open and Billy and JD come running into the kitchen.

MIKE COLLINS
Hey, where were you guys?

BILLY COLLINS
Playing stickball around the corner. JD whacked a good one too!

MIKE COLLINS
Nice going JD. Boys we have to talk about what we're doing on Saturday.

BILLY COLLINS
Dad, don't you remember I have a baseball game at ten?

JD KENDALL
And didn't you say we were going to the robotics show in the city?

MIKE COLLINS
OK, what do you say we go to Billy's game, then White Castle for a sack of belly bombers? After that, we'll head into the city for the robotics show at the Coliseum. How's that sound?

EMILY COLLINS
Mike, can't you think of something better for the three of you to eat than White Castle?

MIKE COLLINS
What's wrong with White Castle? It's got three of the four food groups covered. You got your pickles, onions and ketchup, that's the vegetables. Then for your grains you got the bun and finally the meat which is a good dose of protein.

EMILY COLLINS
You're incorrigible, you know that?

JD KENDALL
What's incorrigible mean?

MIKE COLLINS
(tapping his temple)
It means I'm smart.

BILLY COLLINS
That you are pop!

EMILY COLLINS
(exasperated)
Oh brother!

Emily unties her apron throws it over a kitchen chair and retreats to the living room to read her Ladies Home Journal.

MIKE COLLINS
Boys, you're old enough now that you should be thinking about what you want to do with your lives. Have you given it any thought?

BILLY COLLINS
Well, between what you and grandpa told me about being a cop, I was thinking about carrying on the tradition. I'd go to school and all, but I see the way people admire you when you're in uniform dad.

MIKE COLLINS
That's true, but it's not as glamorous as you think. If you really wanna do it, I'll support you all the way through. Couldn't hurt being a Collins boy either. How 'bout you JD?

JD KENDALL
Well, I really like designing and building things, so something like that.

MIKE COLLINS

Well there are some really great schools for those kinds of careers. There's one up in Boston called MIT. That's where the really smart kids go. I'll stop by the library and ask around the precinct, see what I can come up with. Whattya think?

JD KENDALL

Wow! a college where you design and build things. Cool!

MIKE COLLINS

Alright boys, so we're set for Saturday?
(to Emily around the corner)
Hey Em, I'm going down to McGuinty's for a pint. What time is dinner?

EMILY COLLINS

Six o'clock. Chicken and potatoes, green beans and apple pie.

MIKE COLLINS

Sounds good, I'll see you guys at six.
(to the boys)
Don't tear up the house while I'm gone.

Mike turns and heads out the back door.

JD KENDALL

So, whattya wanna do?

BILLY COLLINS

I don't know what do you wanna do?

JD KENDALL

We could do Rock 'em Sock 'em Robots, play electric football or how bout we make a really big bubble with Super Elastic Bubble Plastic?

BILLY COLLINS

Yeah, Let's Go!

#

Title: "Bar Scene 1"

Source: "Exacting Retribution" *Feature Script*

Genre: Drama

Tone: Light

Approx. Length: 3 Minutes

Character 1: Roy Ingram - *Male, 40's*

Character 2: Sam Vargas - *Male, 50's*

Scene Description:
City bar, present day.

ROY INGRAM

Evening Sam. How's life treating you?

SAM VARGAS

Painfully, that's why I'm here.

ROY INGRAM

Rough day in the salt mines?

SAM VARGAS

It started out OK, and then quickly turned to shit when my boss decided to punish me after I rejected her advances at the company's holiday party.

ROY INGRAM

Why? Is she a beast?

SAM VARGAS

Hardly. Picture a tall brunette with a body built like a brick shithouse. Kind of broad that stops clocks and causes guys to fall off ladders.

ROY INGRAM
So, a beauty like that, why didn't you take her up on her offer?

SAM VARGAS
Roy, I learned a long time ago. You don't taste your honey where you get your money.

ROY INGRAM
Putting it that way buddy, I agree. But, what made it turn to shit?

SAM VARGAS
Let's just say that with one sentence out of her mouth, I got a $100,000 pay cut.

ROY INGRAM
Ouch. You telling me she can get away with that? Can't you report her to HR for that crap?

SAM VARGAS
I could go that route, but I'm envisioning some-thing a little more sinister, just don't know how to go about it though. Maybe this drink will help lubricate the thought process.

ROY INGRAM
Sam, let me take care of those guys over there and I'll be right back. I might have a solution to your problem.

Roy goes to the other end of the bar, pours two drafts, goes to the register and heads back to Sam. With his elbows on the bar, Roy leans in close to Sam.

ROY INGRAM
(whispers)

Sam, I know some people who can discreetly handle that situation. They're very effective.

SAM VARGAS

Really? Like what and how much will that set me back?

ROY INGRAM

Well, if you're interested, I'll get them in touch with you. But understand this Sam, it's all or nothing. Once it starts rolling, you can't pull the plug. And as far as payment, expect to perform occasional favors if you are called on.

Think it over and let me know.

SAM VARGAS

Make it happen.
#

Title: "Airport Scene"

Source: "Exacting Retribution" *Feature Script*

Genre: Drama

Tone: Light

Approx. Length: 2 Minutes

Character 1: Port Authority Cop **-** *Male, 50's*

Character 2: Valerie Webster - *Female, 40's*

Scene Description:
TSA screening area, present day.

PORT AUTHORITY COP
Excuse me miss is this your bag?

VALERIE WEBSTER
Yes, Officer. Is there a problem?

PORT AUTHORITY COP
I'm going to have to place you under arrest.

VALERIE WEBSTER
Under arrest? For what?

PORT AUTHORITY COP
Possession of a loaded firearm in an airport
facility and transportation of an illegal substance.

VALERIE WEBSTER
You've got to be fucking kidding me! I don't own a
frigging gun, and I'm sure as hell not a drug mule.

PORT AUTHORITY COP
You have the right to remain silent. Anything you
say can be used against you in a court of law. You
have a right to have an attorney present during
questioning. If you cannot afford an attorney, one
will be appointed to you. Do you understand your
rights as I've explained them to you?

VALERIE WEBSTER
Yes officer, I've seen more than enough cop
shows in my life. Just tell me where the fuck you're
taking me!

PORT AUTHORITY COP
You'll be held at our precinct, pending investiga-
tion. Then transported to Queens Central Booking,
and then to the Queens House of Detention to
await your hearing before a judge.

VALERIE WEBSTER
How long will all of that take?

PORT AUTHORITY COP
All depends on how many other arrests are in the
system ahead of you, but I guarantee you won't be
leaving the area soon.

VALERIE WEBSTER
This is utter fucking bullshit.
                (to the onlookers)
What the fuck are you people looking at? Mind
your own goddamn business.
#

Title: "Bar Scene 2"

Source: "Exacting Retribution" *Feature Script*

Genre: Drama

Tone: Light

Approx. Length: 2 Minutes

Character 1: Roy Ingram **-** *Male, 40's*

Character 2: Bar Patron - *Male, 30's*

Scene Description:
City bar, present day.

ROY INGRAM

What can I get you pal?

BAR PATRON

Gimme a double bourbon on the rocks with a
loaded pistol chaser.

ROY INGRAM

OK, I know where the drink goes, but I'm curious
who the gun's gonna be aimed at.

BAR PATRON

I haven't decided if I'm gonna eat the bullet, or
feed it to my psycho girlfriend. Either way, my
head's gonna clear up.

ROY INGRAM

Sounds drastic if you ask me. Why you going that
extreme?

BAR PATRON

Listen, she's not your average woman. She's a goddamn freak in the sack. There isn't anything she won't do. You name it, she's game.

ROY INGRAM

Sounds like there's a "but" coming.

BAR PATRON

You think I'd need the gun if it was just that?

When we ain't in the sack, it's like walking past a mean and hungry junkyard dog that's a busted chain link away from ripping your throat out.

ROY INGRAM

Here's my suggestion, take it or leave it. Run outta that house like it was on fire, and get your rocks off elsewhere. That way you avoid being some guy's jail bitch and prevents your family from sponging your brains off the wall.

BAR PATRON

Thanks, but I wish it was that easy.
#

Title: "Simon Mifflin"

Source: "Exacting Retribution" *Feature Script*

Genre: Drama

Tone: Light

Approx. Length: 9 Minutes

Character 1: JD Kendall - *Male, 40's*

Character 2: Roy Ingram - *Male, 40's*

Character 3: Lisa - *Female, 30's*

Character 3: Simon Mifflin - *Male, 50's*

Character 4: Mrs. Mifflin - *Female, 50's*

Scene Description:
Office, bank and suburban home present day.

JD KENDALL

Lisa how are you today? We're two old college
buddies of Simon, and we want to surprise him.
Is he on the phone now?

LISA

No, he just got off a call.

JD KENDALL

Excellent, we're going to kidnap him for lunch,
what do you think?

LISA

That sounds great. Have fun.

JD KENDALL

Oh, we will.

SIMON MIFFLIN
(startled)
Hey, who are you guys and what are you doing
here?

JD KENDALL
Mr. Mifflin, right now there is a gentleman sitting in
a van outside your house ready to deliver flowers
to your lovely wife Angela and another man is at
the park watching your daughter Hayley playing on
the slide.

Now, do as I say, and your wife will get flowers
and a romantic note from you and your daughter
Laurie will continue to play blissfully in the park. If
you choose to ignore me, I will direct both men to
do otherwise. I'm waiting for an answer Mr. Mifflin.

SIMON MIFFLIN
What is it you want from me?

ROY INGRAM
Seven Hundred and Fifty Thousand dollars to be
exact.

SIMON MIFFLIN
I...I don't have that kind of money.

JD KENDALL
Wrong answer Mr. Mifflin.

JD pulls out his phone, hits speed dial and listens.

JD KENDALL
Oh, how precious she's on the swings now.

SIMON MIFFLIN
Wait...Wait, I can get it, but it will take some time.

JD KENDALL
The more time you take Mr. Mifflin, the harder this
will get on you and your family. Do I make myself
clear?

SIMON MIFFLIN
Yes, perfectly. How will I get in touch with you?

JD KENDALL
Mr. Mifflin, do we look like amateurs to you?

The three of us are going for a ride. Piss me off
again and I hit speed dial, this time with a dire
outcome. Comprendo Senor Mifflin?

SIMON MIFFLIN
Yes

JD KENDALL
Very good. Now, hand over your phone and keys,
walk out the door, and follow our conversation until
we're in the car.

So Simon, have you heard from Ted Sheckler or
Mindy Sussman, I understand they recently be-
came an item.

SIMON MIFFLIN
No I didn't hear that. Excuse me a second.
(to Lisa)
We're going out to lunch, I'll be back soon.

LISA
I know, isn't that great. Have fun you guys!

ROY INGRAM
So Simon, I'm up for a steak at Morton's how 'bout you?

JD KENDALL
O.K., Where to Mr. Mifflin? Remember, you're not leaving us till there is seven hundred fifty thousand dollars in cash in this duffel bag, so let's get a move on.

SIMON MIFFLIN
Do you know the Bank of America branch on the corner of Wilson and Jardine? I have a safety deposit box there, I can get some of the money.

JD KENDALL
Don't toy with me. How much?

SIMON MIFFLIN
About four hundred thousand or so.

JD KENDALL
That's a start. Now it goes without saying that I will accompany you into the bank to prevent you from doing or saying anything stupid.

JD KENDALL

To make sure you follow my directions, I'm
attaching a remote control electroshock pad
to your chest.

One false move and everyone around you will
gasp in horror as you clutch your chest and fall to
the ground in a grand mal seizure. And this cute
lapel pin I'm adorning you with is a wireless
microphone so I can hear your slightest whisper.

Any questions Mr. Mifflin?

SIMON MIFFLIN

Wait...wait, I do have a question. Who are you
working for and why are you doing this to me?

JD KENDALL

After you've successfully completed your mission
Mr. Mifflin, all will be revealed.

JD KENDALL

Mr. Mifflin, would you like me to test the pad on
you before going inside?

SIMON MIFFLIN

No, that won't be necessary; you've made your
point very clear.

JD KENDALL

Excellent. Now before you go, here is a refresher
course in the event you decide to cross me.

I will be following a few paces behind you, but if I
see, hear or sense anything out of the ordinary
from you before, during or after you leave the
bank, I will activate the electroshock pad and then
make two very important phone calls.

Are we in agreement that it's in your family's best
interest to do the right thing Mr. Mifflin?

                    SIMON MIFFLIN
Yes, we are in agreement.

                    JD KENDALL
So, what are you waiting for Mr. Mifflin, banks
don't have carhops, the money won't come out to
you.

TIME CUT

                    JD KENDALL
Well Mr. Mifflin, three hundred fifty thousand to go.
Do I have to remind you that I have associates
eagerly awaiting my call or are you going to tell us,
without prompting, where we might collect
the balance?

                    SIMON MIFFLIN
I'm thinking, please give me a minute.

                    JD KENDALL
Don't think too hard Mr. Mifflin, you'll hurt yourself.

You've got sixty seconds from...mark, then I dispatch the flower delivery man to take your wife's
breath away.

SIMON MIFFLIN
O.K., O.K. I have the rest of the money in a safe at home. After I give you that, will you leave me and my family alone?

JD KENDALL
If you follow my final set of directions and your bill is paid in full, yes Mr. Mifflin I promise we will leave you alone.

SIMON MIFFLIN
What is it that you want me to do?

JD KENDALL
Call your wife and tell her that she has to take the Mercedes down to the dealership right away because you were just notified about a hazardous defect in the car's braking system.

JD KENDALL
Go on Mr. Mifflin, sell it to her.

SIMON MIFFLIN
Hi honey, listen the dealership just contacted me. You have to take the car down there right away there's a defect in the brakes.

MRS. MIFFLIN
Can it wait? I'm in the middle of planting my zinnias by the gazebo.

SIMON MIFFLIN
The landscape work can wait. I don't want anything bad to happen to you or Laurie.

MRS. MIFFLIN
What time do they close?

SIMON MIFFLIN
I don't know, but they said first come, first served,
so if you leave now you'll get out sooner.

MRS. MIFFLIN
I guess you're right. OK, give me a few minutes to
clean up and then I'll go.

SIMON MIFFLIN
Thank you. I'll talk to you later.

JD KENDALL
Mr. Mifflin, I thought you'd like to know that the
flower delivery man will follow your wife, and upon
my instruction will involve her in a nasty multi-car
accident if you fail to do the right thing. Do I make
myself clear?

SIMON MIFFLIN
Yes sir, I understand.

JD KENDALL
Let's proceed Mr. Mifflin, time's a wasting.

JD KENDALL
OK Mr. Mifflin, step backwards from the safe with
your hands in the air.

SIMON MIFFLIN
You're not going to shoot me are you?

JD KENDALL

Today is your lucky day Mr. Mifflin, I brought my gun but forgot to bring the bullets. Now step back to the chair or I'll drop you right where you stand.

Mr. Mifflin, I suggest from this day forward, you refrain from scamming people. You never know if and when it will bite you squarely in the ass, as we've just shown you.

And, don't forget. If you fail to follow the straight and narrow, we'll be forced to revisit your life. Would you like see that come to fruition Mr. Mifflin?

SIMON MIFFLIN
(bound & gagged)

MMMMRRRR!

JD KENDALL

I'll take that as a resounding no. Very well then. Enjoy the rest of your day Mr. Mifflin, don't get up, we'll see ourselves out.
#

Title: "Park Scene"

Source: "Exacting Retribution" *Feature Script*

Genre: Drama

Tone: Light

Approx. Length: 4 Minutes

Character 1: JD Kendall **-** *Male, 40's*

Character 2: Linda Morelli - *Female, 40's*

Character 3: Boy at Event - *Male, 12*

Scene Description:
Park event, present day.

LINDA MORELLI

Mr. Kendall, I can't thank you enough for putting this event together and inviting us to chaperone the children.

JD KENDALL

Please call me JD.

LINDA MORELLI
(shaking hands)

Linda Morelli. I work over at the Eight-Eight in Brooklyn, Missing Persons unit. When I heard from my girlfriend in the One Twelve Forest Hills about the event, I volunteered to help out.

JD KENDALL

Well thank you very much for volunteering your time for our kids. You won't be disappointed.

LINDA MORELLI

I'm ready to get started, what do you need me to do?

- 41 -

JD KENDALL

Well if you don't mind, I could use some help here
signing items in and out, that would be a great.

LINDA MORELLI

So tell me about yourself. Have you been in the
hobby business a long time?

JD KENDALL

Well, I was up at MIT when my father was killed on
the job. I left to take care of my mother and
needing a bone to chew, I found a hobby shop
who's owner was retiring. I renovated the location,
upgraded the product selection and the rest is
history.

LINDA MORELLI

How did you come up with the idea to do an event
like this?

JD KENDALL

I wanted to give back to those that deserve it.
Wealthy clients come in with their spoiled brats,
they get whatever they want, and rarely say thank
you. Here you have kids that appreciate the
smallest gesture. Some of them can't say it,
but you see it in their eyes.

LINDA MORELLI

Growing up, we weren't poor, but we weren't rich
either. At least there was love in the house and
food on the table. Something I rarely see out there
these days.

JD KENDALL
Been on the job a long time?

LINDA MORELLI
19 down, one to go. My uncle worked Bronx ESU
in the 70's. Always seemed larger than life to me.

I walked a beat in Brooklyn for a while, took every
test under the sun, worked my ass off, and now
I'm Detective Second Grade.

JD KENDALL
So, do you love what you do?

LINDA MORELLI
It's sad when a young child goes missing like Etan
Patz or John Walsh's kid. When you know or have
a feeling that it's an abduction by an estranged
parent, it's less traumatic. We see people on a
daily basis, who want us to instantly mobilize the
entire police force to find their missing family
members.

JD KENDALL
Do you take it home with you, or have you learned
to shut it off?

LINDA MORELLI
Some of these cases will get to you no matter
what.

BOY AT EVENT
Excuse me sir, the wheel broke on my car, it really
wasn't my fault.

JD KENDALL

Oh, that's alright, I can fix it at my shop. Here take this one, you'll like it.

BOY AT EVENT

Thank you sir.

JD KENDALL

See what I mean?

LINDA MORELLI

Yeah. So JD, what do you do for fun?

JD KENDALL

The shop keeps me busy enough, other than that I tinker around trying to come up with new ideas. Why do you ask?

LINDA MORELLI

I'd love to come by the shop sometime, it sounds like a fun place.

JD KENDALL

Yes, for many of us it is.
#

Title: "Phone Scam"

Source: "Exacting Retribution" *Feature Script*

Genre: Drama

Tone: Light

Approx. Length: 2 Minutes

Character 1: JD Kendall - *Male, 40's*

Character 2: Rodney Ellington - *Male, 20's*

Scene Description:
Telephone scam. Character 1 uses announcer's voice, Character 2 street slang.

                    JD KENDALL
Rodney Ellington, this is Dave West from the promotions department of Power 99. I'm calling to congratulate you on being selected our Grand Prize Winner in Power 99's Grand Vegas Giveaway.

The prize package includes a stretch limo to the airport, first class tickets to Las Vegas where you'll stay at the sumptuous Bellagio Hotel, plus one thousand dollars in cold hard cash, all from your friends at Power 99. But, and you know there's a but Rodney. You need to call my private line at 666-6699 by midnight tonight in order to claim your amazing prize package worth over five thousand dollars. If we don't hear from you by midnight, the trip and the cash, all of it goes to the runner-up. It's all on you Rodney. Make that call and head off to Vegas, courtesy of your friends at Power 99!

TIME CUT

JD KENDALL

Dave West, Power 99

RODNEY ELLINGTON

Yea, uh this is Rodney. I'm claimin' my piece of Vegas.

JD KENDALL

That's the attitude Rodney! OK, first off, I need to verify your address so that we can send a stretch limousine to pick you up. You are available, no work or family conflicts right?

RODNEY ELLINGTON

Hells no. Even if there was, ain't nothing gonna stop me from goin to Vegas baby. Send that limo to my crib at 44A Clermont Avenue Brooklyn.

JD KENDALL

Atta boy Rodney! Start packing. The stretch limo will be there tomorrow at 9AM to take you away from here. Enjoy your trip and don't forget to tell em' Power 99 sent you!

RODNEY ELLINGTON

You damm skippy on that.
#

Title: "Phone Banter"

Source: "Exacting Retribution" *Feature Script*

Genre: Drama

Tone: Light

Approx. Length: 3 Minutes

Character 1: JD Kendall - *Male, 40's*

Character 2: Linda Morelli - *Female, 40's*

Scene Description:
Phone call, present day.

JD KENDALL

Detective Morelli, so nice to hear from you.

LINDA MORELLI

JD, I hope all is well with you since we last saw each other at your event.

JD KENDALL

Busy but good, can't complain.

LINDA MORELLI

Well, I hope this isn't short notice for you, but today is my RDO and my son is at a sleepover, so I thought we could have dinner tonight and afterwards you could give me a tour of your shop.

JD KENDALL

Dinner sounds great, but what is an RDO?

LINDA MORELLI

RDO is cop speak for regular day off.

JD KENDALL

Ah sorry, I should have figured that one out. So, what's your poison? Denny's, Chuck E. Cheese, Waffle House?

LINDA MORELLI

Very funny wise guy. I want a nice red sauce Italian dinner, just like Ma used to make every Sunday. You're not allergic to tomatoes are you?

JD KENDALL

No, just idiots and rude people. I know just the place. Can you be ready by eight?

LINDA MORELLI

Not a problem. Are you gonna tell me where you're taking me or do I have to bring my gun?

JD KENDALL

The island of Manhattan and leave the hardware at home. I'm not the type to abduct someone against their will for nefarious reasons.

LINDA MORELLI

Aw shucks, I guess I won't get lucky tonight then huh?

JD KENDALL

My my Detective, are we a bit frisky tonight?

LINDA MORELLI

Telling it straight comes with the territory Professor.

JD KENDALL

Duly noted Detective Morelli. So, might I coerce an address where I can retrieve you tonight?

LINDA MORELLI

Boy JD you want everything huh?

JD KENDALL

Google Maps and GPS units do a great job, but without entering a destination, they tend to fall a little short.

LINDA MORELLI

Well, punch this in and see where it gets you. 72 Russell Place Edgewater, NJ 06957.

JD KENDALL

Am I picking you up or mailing you a letter? I don't need your zip code.

LINDA MORELLI

Sorry, force of habit, It comes out as one long sentence for me. Do you accept my apology sir?

JD KENDALL

Wear something nice and loose, and I'll let you know. See you at eight.

LINDA MORELLI

And don't be late?

JD KENDALL

If you keep this up, I will be.

LINDA MORELLI

Goodbye JD.

#

Title: "The Date"

Source: "Exacting Retribution" *Feature Script*

Genre: Drama

Tone: Light

Approx. Length: 2 Minutes

Character 1: JD Kendall - *Male, 40's*

Character 2: Linda Morelli - *Female, 40's*

Scene Description:
Residence, present day.

                    JD KENDALL
Well Detective, I must say you wash up quite
nicely.

                    LINDA MORELLI
Aw, Are those flowers for me?

                    JD KENDALL
No, I always walk around with flowers in my hand.

                    LINDA MORELLI
Wiseass, get in here before I change my mind
about you.

                    JD KENDALL
So Linda, you're all by yourself tonight huh, no
kids?

                    LINDA MORELLI
Well, that is unless you start acting like a child and
I have to throw you over my knee and spank you.

                    JD KENDALL
Goo-goo Gaga!

                    LINDA MORELLI
Oh brother, I can see you're going to be a handful.

                    JD KENDALL
Well, to be exact, a little more than a handful.

                    LINDA MORELLI
Don't we have reservations for a red sauce dinner
somewhere in Manhattan or are we gonna banter
like welterweights here in my living room?"

                    JD KENDALL
Yes we do. And to your second question, I'd rather
it take place in the bedroom.

                    LINDA MORELLI
Now who's frisky?

                    JD KENDALL
OK Detective, I surrender. Let me help you with
your coat.

                    LINDA MORELLI
Thank you kind sir.

                    JD KENDALL
My pleasure Miss Morelli. Next stop red sauce.
#

Title: "Restaurant Interrogation"

Source: "Exacting Retribution" *Feature Script*

Genre: Drama

Tone: Light

Approx. Length: 2 Minutes

Character 1: JD Kendall - *Male, 40's*

Character 2: Linda Morelli - *Female, 40's*

Scene Description:
Outside a restaurant, present day.

JD KENDALL

Detective Morelli, what a surprise to see you here.

LINDA MORELLI

Did you have a nice dinner?

JD KENDALL

Are you following me?

LINDA MORELLI

Should I? We got a report of a guy who won a radio contest. A white limo picked him up and he hasn't been heard from since.

JD KENDALL

What does that have to do with me?

LINDA MORELLI

Well I did some digging. Seems like you have a connection to the missing guy.

JD KENDALL

How so?

LINDA MORELLI

Rodney Ellington was the guy who went to trial for killing Officer Billy Collins.

Your stepbrother?

JD KENDALL

And you suspect me in his disappearance? You said the guy went to Vegas.

If I was going there, I wouldn't be calling home every five minutes.

LINDA MORELLI

Fair point, but it's still an odd coincidence that I saw you driving a white stretch.

JD KENDALL

To drop it off for service as a favor to the guy who parks it at the shop.

LINDA MORELLI

I like you JD. I hope you're not dirty, cause if you are, I'm coming after you and it won't be in a nice way.

JD KENDALL

You've got nothing to worry about. I hope you can get past these hunches of yours.

LINDA MORELLI

We'll see JD. We'll see.
#

Title: "Advisor's Office"

Source: "Justified Retribution" *Feature Script*

Genre: Drama

Tone: Light

Approx. Length: 4 Minutes

Character 1: Bill Rothbart - *Male, 50's*

Character 2: Alicia Rogers - *Female, 20's*

Scene Description:
College Advisor's Office, present day.

BILL ROTHBART
Alicia, you didn't have an appointment did you?

ALICIA ROGERS
No, but it's important that I see you. Do you have time for me now?

BILL ROTHBART
Sure, come on in. Is everything alright?

ALICIA ROGERS
Not really that's why I'm here. Something happened a few weeks ago that really can't talk about, and it's preventing me from attending classes.

I want to explore any options where I can complete my degree, but not have to come to class.

BILL ROTHBART
That sounds serious. You sure you don't want to tell me?

ALICIA ROGERS
It is serious, and I'm trying to cope the best I can.

BILL ROTHBART
Alicia, not only am I your advisor, but I think you can trust me as a member of the faculty. And, depending on the issue keep this confidential.

ALICIA ROGERS
I want to trust you, but I'm afraid.

BILL ROTHBART
Afraid of me?

ALICIA ROGERS
No, no. Afraid of what will happen if it gets out.

BILL ROTHBART
You have my solemn word, that whatever it is, it stays between us.

ALICIA ROGERS
I need you to promise me that even after you hear this, nothing will happen.

BILL ROTHBART
I don't know if I can go that far if a crime was committed.

Alicia puts her head in her hands and begins to weep.

BILL ROTHBART
Alicia, what is it?

ALICIA ROGERS
(sobbing)
I was drugged and gang raped by four guys at a frat party.

BILL ROTHBART
Oh my god, I'm so sorry. Did you know who they are; did you report them to campus police?

ALICIA ROGERS
No, don't you see. This can't get out, I'll be dragged thru the mud and never have a chance of practicing law ever.

BILL ROTHBART
But they need to pay for what they did to you.

ALICIA ROGERS
My word against four guys that probably have wealthy lawyers in their daddy's pockets.

Like I said, I can't be dragged thru the mud. Now, can I have your word that this stays right here?

BILL ROTHBART
Against my better judgment as a father, I'll honor your wish. But, I need something in return.

ALICIA ROGERS
(nervous)
What?

BILL ROTHBART

In order for me to help you, I need your word that this meeting and our discussion never occurred. You can imagine the repercussions of not reporting something like this.

ALICIA ROGERS

Wow, it seems we both have something to lose.

So, what are my options?

BILL ROTHBART

Well, the only option is to enroll you in our Distance Learning Program. You'll view lectures, and assignments online, submit work electronically but have to come in and meet with me at least twice per quarter. Does that sound like something you can handle?

ALICIA ROGERS

Definitely. How soon can I start?

BILL ROTHBART

Well, I'll need to get with your professors, then meet with the Distance Learning Department. Don't worry, I'll come up with a viable reason to get you accepted. Should be about a week or so.

ALICIA ROGERS

I've already lost enough time, an extra week shouldn't matter.

BILL ROTHBART

Alicia, I want to help you thru this. If you ever need to talk or run something by me that you're not sure of, feel free to call me.

BILL ROTHBART
Here's my cell number, call me any time.

Are you sure you're alright?

ALICIA ROGERS
I feel better now that I have an alternative. The rest will come in time. I just can't let this kill my chances of finishing my degree after all I've put into it.

BILL ROTHBART
You're already moving in the right direction. Focus on your studies and please, remember to take care of yourself.

ALICIA ROGERS
Thank you so much. I won't forget what you've done for me.

BILL ROTHBART
All I've done is the right thing.
#

Title: "Advisor's Home"

Source: "Justified Retribution" *Feature Script*

Genre: Drama

Tone: Light

Approx. Length: 2 Minutes

Character 1: Bill Rothbart - *Male, 50's*

Character 2: Alicia Rogers - *Female, 20's*

Scene Description:
Phone call to College Advisor's home, present day.

BILL ROTHBART

Hello?

ALICIA ROGERS

It's Alicia, I hope I didn't call too late.

BILL ROTHBART

No, it's alright, I was up reading. Is everything alright?

ALICIA ROGERS

The firm threw me a birthday party at a nice restaurant tonight.

BILL ROTHBART

That was nice of them. Happy Birthday Alicia.

ALICIA ROGERS

Thanks but the real reason I was calling is that I got freaked out on the way home tonight and I felt defenseless. I had to talk to someone about it and I knew you'd understand.

                    BILL ROTHBART
Are you OK now?

                    ALICIA ROGERS
Yes, I'm home, the doors are locked.

                    BILL ROTHBART
When you said you felt defenseless, I had an idea.

                    ALICIA ROGERS
I'm listening.

                    BILL ROTHBART
I want you to look into martial arts training. A good
friend of mine took it up and she claims not only
does she feel in control now but it has helped
center her and build her self esteem. What do you
think?

                    ALICIA ROGERS
I don't know. I always thought it was all about
breaking boards and stuff.

                    BILL ROTHBART
She thought the same thing.

                    ALICIA ROGERS
I'll look into it, thanks again for everything.

                    BILL ROTHBART
Good Night Alicia
#

Title: "Law Office"

Source: "Justified Retribution" *Feature Script*

Genre: Drama

Tone: Light

Approx. Length: 3 Minutes

Character 1: Alicia Rogers **-** *Female, 20's*

Character 2: Tony - *Male, 30's*

Character 3: Jen - *Female, 30's*

Scene Description:
Hallway conversation, present day.

ALICIA ROGERS
Hey Jen, you know anything about martial arts?

JEN
You mean like Kung Fu, Bruce Lee and breaking boards with your hands?

ALICIA ROGERS
Well sorta. What can you tell me?

JEN
I just did. Kung Fu, Bruce Lee and breaking boards with your hands.

TONY
Alicia, don't listen to her. My son Antonio is in a Tae Kwon Do class and it's not all about breaking boards. Before that, he was all hyper and couldn't stay focused. Not ADD, just all over the place. Now you can't believe the difference in him.

ALICIA ROGERS
Really.

TONY
Yea, he's a different kid now. Why do you ask?

ALICIA ROGERS
I wanna start working out and I heard that it was a
good physical and mental workout.

TONY
I totally agree. One of the parents is a black belt
and he swears by it.

ALICIA ROGERS
They have classes for both kids and adults?

TONY
Yea, kids during the day and adults at night.

ALICIA ROGERS
Can you get me the info on this place, I wanna
check it out.

TONY
Here you go, I wrote it down for you.

ALICIA ROGERS
Thanks Tone, I appreciate it.

TIME CUT

ALICIA ROGERS
Hey, Tone. I didn't see you yesterday. I wanted to
tell you I stopped by the do-jang the other night.
Wow, was I impressed.

TONY

I bet. So did you sign up?

ALICIA ROGERS

Yea, the class starts tonight. Already tried on my do-bok. Can't wait to start.

JEN

Hey, you want me to stop off at the lumber yard and pick up some boards for you to break?

ALICIA ROGERS

No, but I wouldn't mind if you picked up my dry cleaning instead.

JEN

Nice try sister, wrong girl.

TONY
(shaking his head)
Always wondered where they found her, at least she's good at what she does.

Anyway, I'm so glad you decided to join, you're gonna love it.

ALICIA ROGERS

Thanks again for the referral. Listen I gotta get movin, too much work, not enough time.

TONY

Tell me about it.
#

Title: "Dojo"

Source: "Justified Retribution" *Feature Script*

Genre: Drama

Tone: Light

Approx. Length: 1 Minute

Character 1: Shoji - Male, 40's

Scene Description:
Martial Arts class, present day.

SHOJI

Good evening everyone, and to our new students, welcome to Hokkaido.

We study the Korean art of Tae Kwon Do. Tae means to strike or break with foot; Kwon means to strike or break with fist; and Do means way, method or art.

So you can say we are studying the art of striking with foot and fist. Not only will you learn basic self defense, you'll also learn self control and gain a feeling of centeredness and well being.

The curriculum will include basic Tae Kwon Do techniques such as sparring, throwing and falling as well as stretching and meditation exercises.

Any questions? Very well. I will pair you off in partners as we begin our stretching exercises. Introduce yourself to your partner and we will begin leg stretches.
#

Title: "Case Meeting"

Source: "Justified Retribution" *Feature Script*

Genre: Drama

Tone: Light

Approx. Length: 2 Minutes

Character 1: Phil Sanders - *Male, 50's*

Character 2: Alicia Rogers - *Female, 20's*

Scene Description:
Law Office, present day.

PHIL SANDERS
Hey Alicia, come on in, have a seat.

ALICIA ROGERS
So I understand I'm second chairing with you, what case are you working on?

PHIL SANDERS
Sherril v Mason County Police Department. Two officers were responding to a Domestic Abuse call where the suspect supposedly had the wife at gun point.

One cop ran a red light and crashed into another vehicle, sending the police car onto a sidewalk full of people.

The Sherril's sixteen year old son James was walking down the sidewalk when the cruiser jumped the curb and crushed him against a building. DOA.

                    ALICIA ROGERS
Oh that poor family.

                    PHIL SANDERS
Yeah, they're pretty shaken up but we can do
some good here.

                    ALICIA ROGERS
How so?

                    PHIL SANDERS
Our researcher found that the driver who ran the
red light has a history of speeding infractions, well
before he was hired on the force.

                    ALICIA ROGERS
So where do I fit in.

                    PHIL SANDERS
Your job is to absorb everything you can here and
in the courtroom. This is your opportunity to be
front and center with limited liability. You ready for
this?

                    ALICIA ROGERS
Absolutely.

                    PHIL SANDERS
Great, here are the case files, take 'em back to
your desk and dive in. We go to court next
Monday, should be enough time to get you up to
speed.

                    ALICIA ROGERS
Thanks
#

Title: "Court 1"

Source: "Justified Retribution" *Feature Script*

Genre: Drama

Tone: Light

Approx. Length: 3 Minutes

Character 1: Phil Sanders **-** *Male, 50's*

Character 2: Alicia Rogers - *Female, 20's*

Character 3: Sal Generoso **-** *Male, 40's*

Character 4: Judge Walsh - *Female, 60's*

Scene Description:
Courthouse, present day.

PHIL SANDERS
Watch how Generoso plays to the jury. If you ever oppose him, make sure you do your homework.

ALICIA ROGERS
Thanks, that's good to know.

SAL GENEROSO
Ladies and Gentlemen of the jury. What happened on June 6th, 2009 was a tragic accident. One that shouldn't have happened, but under the circumstances regretfully did.

Officers and first responders on a daily basis race to the aid of the community, just as Officer Ramon Fuentes and other Officers did on that tragic day.

When you are wrapped up in the moment, your focus is pinpoint. That's what responding officers experience in cases like this.

I ask that you put yourself in Officer Fuentes' position on that day. Getting the call of a domestic situation involving a hostage being held at gunpoint. If you were held at gunpoint, wouldn't you want an immediate response?

All told Ladies and Gentleman this is nothing more than a tragic accident. With that in mind, I trust that you'll find my client Officer Ramon Fuentes, not guilty of the charges before him.

Thank you your honor.

JUDGE WALSH
Ladies and gentlemen of the jury. Due to the late proceedings, we will carry this session over to the day after tomorrow at 9am. This court is adjourned

ALICIA ROGERS
I was impressed how you had him read the abstract, then make him say it was his, rather than you reading it.

PHIL SANDERS
You have to look for ways to take people out of their comfort zone. If you can find something they think you don't know, then spring it on them, you've got them off guard.

ALICIA ROGERS
Duly noted counselor.

PHIL SANDERS

If you don't have to go back to the office, I can
take this stuff back.

ALICIA ROGERS

You sure? That really helps. I have an important
Tae Kwon Do class tonight that I'd like to be ready
for.

PHIL SANDERS

What's important about it?

ALICIA ROGERS

I have a one on one match with my instructor and
if I do well, then I move up in belt rank.

PHIL SANDERS

That sounds exciting. Go kick some ass tonight.

ALICIA ROGERS

Thanks Phil, see you in the morning.
#

Title: "The Four Horsemen"

Source: "Justified Retribution" *Feature Script*

Genre: Drama

Tone: Light

Approx. Length: 13 Minutes

Character 1: Ed Fox - *Male, 30's*

Character 2: Rick Taylor - *Male, 30's*

Character 3: Rocky White - *Male, 30's*

Character 4: Paul Avery - *Male, 30's*

Character 5: Waitress - *Female, 40's*

Scene Description:
Steakhouse, present day.

ED FOX

Good evening boys, sorry I'm late, held up by
boardroom bullshit.

RICK TAYLOR

Sure you weren't just diddling an admin?

ED FOX

No that was before lunch. Listen, thanks for
coming to Jersey this year fellas, seems like
our tight schedules prevented our get together
last year.

ROCKY WHITE

I was knee deep in negotiations with Lexus.
Even if I wanted to break away, I couldn't.

RICK TAYLOR

I had investors breathing down my neck to get a development finished, even though they ignored the friggin' rainstorms from hell.

ED FOX

So Avery, what was your excuse?

PAUL AVERY

The wife.

ED FOX

I'd say Avery wins. That means he hosts next year.

ROCKY WHITE

No offense Fox, but Myrtle Beach will be a welcome relief after being here.

ED FOX

What, you don't like the Garden State?

ROCKY WHITE

Garden? I saw nothing but refineries, cargo containers and swamp flying in here.

ED FOX

That's the area around Newark, you gotta admit Princeton is a bit nicer.

ROCKY WHITE

OK, it does have its share of nubile college girls.

WAITRESS

Good evening gentlemen, welcome to Bison House, my name is Candy, and I'll be serving you tonight.

ED FOX

Candy are you as sweet and tasty as your name implies?

WAITRESS

Now Mr. Fox, is that a nice thing to say before dinner?

ED FOX

Well, how bout after dinner?

WAITRESS
(demurring)
Gentlemen, what can I get you to drink?

ROCKY WHITE

Are you on the drink menu?

Hmm, not a peep. Alright, let me have a large bourbon and water darlin' minus the water.

RICK TAYLOR

Dry martini, no olive.

PAUL AVERY

Bud Lite please.

WAITRESS

And you Mr. Fox?

ED FOX

I'll take a Jameson's neat.

WAITRESS

Very well gentlemen, I'll be back shortly.

ROCKY WHITE

I'd do her in a heartbeat.

PAUL AVERY

Rock, there could be a hole in the wall with a sign above it that said insert here and you'd do that too.

ROCKY WHITE

It would have to be a tight hole, I have standards you know.

ED FOX

So Rock, how many dealerships are you up to now?

ROCKY WHITE

Three Mercedes, one with Maybach, two Lexus and one each for BMW, Jaguar, Land Rover and Mini. The latest Lexus shop is in the next town over from me.

RICK TAYLOR

Not bad, last time we got together, you didn't have the Mini or the Maybach yet.

ROCKY WHITE

Life is good boys, life is good.

WAITRESS
Here you go gentlemen, let me know when you're ready to order.

ROCKY WHITE
Drinks? Just keep 'em coming.

WAITRESS
Well that too, but I meant entrees.

ED FOX
Give us a few minutes.

WAITRESS
No problem Mr. Fox.

RICK TAYLOR
She does have a nice ass.

ED FOX
I see none of you have lost your edge. Except Avery with his lite beer.

Here's a toast to the Four Horsemen!

ALL FOUR
Hoo Rah!

ED FOX
We were a force to be reckoned with back then. Different playing field now, but I'd say we all turned out well.

Healthy, wealthy, families for some, and still no regrets.

And here's to our conquests!

ALL FOUR
Hoo Rah!

ROCKY WHITE
That's the part I'd like to re-live.

PAUL AVERY
You guys ever wonder what happened to any of
them?

RICK TAYLOR
They've probably become overweight soccer
moms driving minivans and poppin' Zanax like it
was Pez.

ED FOX
Any of them stick out for you boys?

ROCKY WHITE
Didn't remember much after we were finished with
em.

PAUL AVERY
Now that I've got a daughter of my own, I see it
from a different point of view.

Don't get me wrong, we had a blast, but things are
different now.

ROCKY WHITE
Defector Alert! Defector Alert!

RICK TAYLOR

Enough Rock, you're a bachelor for life you'll never understand.

ED FOX

Boys, boys, let's not get soft in our old age. Some of us may have changed but deep down we're still the rutting dogs we used to be.

Here comes the waitress, you guys ready to order?

ROCKY WHITE

Hell yeah, the aroma of seared beef coming from the other tables is killing me.

WAITRESS

Ready to order gentlemen?

ED FOX

I'll have a Porterhouse medium rare and a baked potato.

RICK TAYLOR

The largest lobster you have back there, drowning in butter.

ROCKY WHITE

Cowboy Rib eye, bleedin' on the inside, blackened on the outside and I'll take a tater also.

WAITRESS

You want tater tots?

ROCKY WHITE

Do I look like a five year old to you darlin? If so, you could be my older woman fantasy tonight.

WAITRESS

And what can I get for you sir?

PAUL AVERY

I'll take the grilled chicken breast, mixed steamed vegetables on the side.

WAITRESS

Very well gentlemen, I'll be back with another round of drinks shortly.

ROCKY WHITE

You have gone soft. Lite beer, grilled chicken and steamed veggies?

Boys, we should have a wake for the old Avery. Let's bow our heads in memory of our dearly departed friend Paul Avery, who seems to have lost his spine and his manhood to the ravaging scourge of domesticity.

RICK TAYLOR

Cut it out Rock

PAUL AVERY

Yeah, you double wide trailer trash Texan, it's not as bad as you think.

ROCKY WHITE

Maybe so, but it sure as hell ain't for me.

TIME CUT

ROCKY WHITE
You know what would make this one of the best
meals ever?

ED FOX
What would that be Rock?

ROCKY WHITE
A foursome under this table polishing our knobs.

ED FOX
I didn't see that on the menu, but we could always
get dessert after we leave here.

ROCKY WHITE
Now you're talkin Fox.

RICK TAYLOR
I wouldn't mind a cigar after this.

PAUL AVERY
Never acquired the taste.

WAITRESS
Is everything alright here?

ED FOX
Just fine Candy.

WAITRESS
Can I get you boys some dessert?

They all chuckle at the irony.

ED FOX

No Candy, I think we'll be eating out later. But, I'll take the check as soon as you're ready.

WAITRESS

Very well, any drinks before I settle up?

ED FOX

Why not add one last round to the check before you close it

WAITRESS

No problem, coming right up.

ROCKY WHITE

Jesus, when she said that, I thought I was gonna spit my Bourbon across the table.

PAUL AVERY

Had I known that, I would have grabbed a lighter just to see you spit fire like a circus freak.

ROCKY WHITE

Who you callin a circus freak?

PAUL AVERY

Wow, you can dish it but you can't take it huh?

RICK TAYLOR

Rock, are you that wasted? He didn't call you a circus freak. Although you have potential...

ROCKY WHITE
Why you...

ED FOX
Alright are you kids gonna cut it out, or do I have
to stop the car.

RICK TAYLOR
Sorry dad..

WAITRESS
OK boys, last round and Mr. Fox I'll take the check
from you when you're ready.

ED FOX
One second, I'll take care of it right now.

WAITRESS
Thank you sir, I'll be right back.

ED FOX
OK boys, peel off some large denomination dead
presidents for the nice lady, finish these drinks and
then we head out for dessert.

RICK TAYLOR
Sweet.

ROCKY WHITE
Oh, I almost forgot. This is a good one.

Who's Irish and sits around the backyard all
summer?

PAUL AVERY

I heard that one when I was eleven Rock. Patio
Furniture. Please stick to selling cars and promise
us you won't go anywhere near a comedy stage.

ROCKY WHITE

Well, I thought it was funny when I heard it.

ED FOX

Car accidents are funny to you Rock. Let's go
boys, drink up, I'm ready for some dessert.

WAITRESS

Gentlemen it was a pleasure serving you tonight
and Mr. Fox it's always a pleasure having you
here at the Bison House.

ED FOX

Thank you Candy.

WAITRESS

Enjoy the rest of your evening.

ROCKY WHITE

Oh, we will darlin, we will.

The boys get up, walk out and White burps loudly.

ROCKY WHITE

Ah, now I have enough room for dessert.

PAUL AVERY

Rock, did you ever realize that when your drunk
you really turn into an uncouth asshole?
#

Title: "Court 2"

Source: "Justified Retribution" *Feature Script*

Genre: Drama

Tone: Light

Approx. Length: 2 Minutes

Character 1: Dennis Jenkins - *Male, 30's*

Character 2: Alicia Rogers - *Female, 30's*

Character 3: Judge Kendrick - *Female, 60's*

Scene Description:
Courthouse, present day.

DENNIS JENKINS

Ladies and Gentlemen of the jury, I ask that you remain cognizant of the facts presented in this case as you deliberate.

All of the necessary food safety measures were and continue to be in place at my client's manufacturing facilities.

Any transient, airborne or outside contaminants are strictly screened and monitored on a regular basis. In the event that an unknown contaminant enters the production cycle at any point in time, spot testing of final product in my client's labs will raise caution and stop production.

In conclusion, my client's company has followed strict USDA and OSHA guidelines to the letter and will continue to diligently manufacture quality food products.

The defense rests your honor.

ALICIA ROGERS

Imagine that you are a parent of a happy and healthy 12 year old boy, who also happens to have a preventable life threatening food allergy.

You are diligent in what he eats and expect that food manufacturers are just as diligent in their standards for safety.

Your son can safely eat his favorite cookies Yummy O's. That is until the last box of those Yummy-O's you bought was produced on a contaminated production line.

Ladies and gentlemen, by contaminated, I don't mean radiation, pesticides or something like that.

All it takes to contaminate a sterilized production line is a trace of an allergen. In this case the allergen was milk.

12 year old Anthony Hughes' milk protein allergy is a five on a scale of six. Life threatening.

Imagine if you will your son helps himself to a stack of Yummy-O's as he always does, but this time, he goes into anaphylactic shock.

Busy in the basement washing clothes, You're unaware that your son was gasping for his last breath right above you.

I ask you in that same frame of mind as a parent. Would you leave here satisfied after hearing Standard Bakery's scripted apology for errors that caused the death of that 12 year old boy?

If not, I trust that you will side with my clients, providing them with the closure they and their late 12 year old son Anthony Hughes rightly deserve.

Thank You

The prosecution rests your honor.

JUDGE KENDRICK

Members of the jury, you have heard all the evidence as well as the arguments of the attorneys. Now it is up to you to deliberate the verdict.

If you find for the prosecution you must also determine reasonable compensation. The jury is excused for deliberations, court is adjourned.
#

Title: "Avery's Demise"

Source: "Justified Retribution" *Feature Script*

Genre: Drama

Tone: Dark

Approx. Length: 4 Minutes

Character 1: Paul Avery **-** *Male, 30's*

Character 2: Alicia Rogers - *Female, 30's*

Scene Description:
Suburban house, present day.

ALICIA ROGERS

Calm down or I'll snap your neck and kill you right here. You will listen clearly and do as I say. Do you understand?

PAUL AVERY

Who are you? If you want money, I'll get it for you, just don't hurt me.

ALICIA ROGERS

Shut up and walk towards the garage. Try anything stupid, and I'll drop you right where you stand.

ALICIA ROGERS

Thought you could break loose huh? Well dipshit, here's a news flash. I let you go, so I could kick your ass.

Oh, does that hurt tough guy? Digest that kick, I'll be right back.

PAUL AVERY
(screaming)
Who are you and what do you want?

ALICIA ROGERS
Shut up asshole, I can't hear the music.

INT. AVERY'S HOUSE - GARAGE - DAY

ALICIA ROGERS
Damn, I should have dragged you by your feet.
That way I could've watched your coconut go
gdunk,gdunk then boom on the floor.

Now stand up.

PAUL AVERY
I can't. You broke my leg.

ALICIA ROGERS
You want a matching set? Get up!

PAUL AVERY
(beaten)
You think your tough? My friends will hunt you
down, then you're as good as dead. You don't
know what you're dealing with here.

ALICIA ROGERS
Put a sock in it, or would you rather I kick your
teeth in so you have a final meal?

So, punching bag, do you know who I am?

PAUL AVERY

A very sick bitch.

ALICIA ROGERS

You and your friends made me this way asshole.
Let me refresh your memory.

Alpha Delta Theta. Pommel Horse. Gang Bang. Is
it coming to you yet?

PAUL AVERY

You're just one of many we did, doesn't matter.

ALICIA ROGERS

Speaking of we, tell me who else was involved
that night.

PAUL AVERY

I forgot.

ALICIA ROGERS

Wrong answer stupid. Time for you to make like a
goldfish in this here bag and take your last breath.

So tough guy, won't be much longer till you
suffocate. Love to stay till the bitter end, but
I'm off to pay a visit to the other three.

I really can't wait to tell them how you let a girl kick
your ass.
#

Title: "White's Demise"

Source: "Justified Retribution" *Feature Script*

Genre: Drama

Tone: Dark

Approx. Length: 5 Minutes

Character 1: Rocky White - *Male, 30's*

Character 2: Alicia Rogers - *Female, 30's*

Scene Description:
Car Interior, then woods, present day.

ROCKY WHITE

Listen, I just got firebombed at my new Lexus dealership. It's gotta be that woman coming after us. If you find her, I want a piece of that bitch. She just cost me a fortune.

Yea, I know. I'll keep my eyes out for her. Bye.

ALICIA ROGERS

I can easily put two rounds in your head before you realize what hit you. Now do as I say and follow the GPS.

ROCKY WHITE

If you want money...

ALICIA ROGERS

I have more than enough of my own thanks, now shut up and no stupid moves or my accomplice will set fire to your house and pick off anything fleeing the inferno. Do I have your attention now?

ROCKY WHITE

Yes, but what is it you want darlin? You name it,
it's yours.

ALICIA ROGERS

I'm not your darlin and I'll say it slower this time
cause you're a fucking hillbilly idiot.

Follow the friggin GPS. The next time I have to tell
you, I put a round in your leg. Now get going and
remember dumb shit equals dead burning dogs.
Got it?

ROCKY WHITE

Who are you?

ALICIA ROGERS

You stole something from me, now it's time to take
it back.

ROCKY WHITE

Oh, you're that bitch that took Avery out. He was a
lightweight.

You may think you have the upper hand just cause
you have a gun pointed at me, but you're not
gettin off that easy with me.

ALICIA ROGERS

Enough of the fairy tales dumbass. Shut up and
drive before I get a spasm in my trigger finger
and paint the interior with your brains.

ALICIA ROGERS

Pull up to the left side of the silver pickup truck
and remember no stupid shit or dogs on fire
become target practice

Now, put those handcuffs on and get out of the car
when I say so.

ROCKY WHITE

What if I refuse?

ALICIA ROGERS

Boy you are dense. Bullet to your head then
dogs get matching high powered rounds to their
heads.

Now put the goddamn cuffs on!

OK, get out, stand up, and take one step forward
and two steps to the left. Can you handle that?

ROCKY WHITE

You think you're tough shit huh? Avery was a
pushover. I can kick your ass even with these
cuffs on.

ALICIA ROGERS

OK dumbass, I could use a workout. Bring it on.

Nice try overweight, stupid and out of shape.

ROCKY WHITE

What are you going to do, leave me here chained
up?

ALICIA ROGERS
No, you're gonna visit the chiropractor as soon as
you get your fat ass up and outta the mud piggie.
Remember, I can call my associate if you need a
little motivation, or just put a round in your leg.
What's it gonna be?

Good boy, now walk over to the back of the pickup
truck, I'll let the gun at the back of your head guide
you if you slow down or get lost.

OK, on your knees and grab the trailer hitch like it
was the best girl you never had.

ROCKY WHITE
What are you gonna do to me?

ALICIA ROGERS
Oh, I don't know, visualize it for yourself. Alicia
walks back to a tree and drags back a chain and
attaches it to White's leg irons.

ROCKY WHITE
(pleading)
Listen, It wasn't my idea. Ya gotta believe me.
This was all Fox's idea.

ALICIA ROGERS
I could give a shit who's idea it was. You all were
there, you all go down. And can ya guess what I
have in store for you tonight?

(Southern Dialect)

You're gonna make like a hammock stretched between that there tree and this here pickup. Only thing is, I'm gonna drive that pickup outta here.

So the question of the day is, where ya gonna snap in two? And, on that note, it's time to get a move on. See ya later stretch!
#

Title: "Taylor's Demise"

Source: "Justified Retribution" *Feature Script*

Genre: Drama

Tone: Dark

Approx. Length: 6 Minutes

Character 1: Rick Taylor - *Male, 30's*

Character 2: Alicia Rogers - *Female, 30's*

Character 3: Taylor's Guy #1 - *Male, 20's*

Character 4: Taylor's Guy #2 - *Male, 20's*

Scene Description:
Suburban basement, present day.

RICK TAYLOR

Well, well we meet again. We figured one of the women we hosted might eventually come back. Pissed, maybe even with a lawsuit, but we never figured one of them might actually have the guts to take us on.

Let's see, you hogtied and suffocated Avery, firebombed White's dealership and now what did you have planned for me?

Well, sorry I thwarted your plans. Oh by the way, we grabbed your boy the other day as he was walking home from school. Nice kid I hear.

ALICIA ROGERS
(livid)
You son of a bitch. This is strictly between me and each one of you assholes. My kid gets hurt or harmed in any way, I'll torture you nice and slow, bury you half alive, piss all over you, then dig you up and kick your sorry ass all over again.

RICK TAYLOR
(laughing)
Keep an eye on her boys, I gotta go upstairs and make a call before I partake in our guest one last time.
TAYLOR'S GUY #1
You think she's secure enough that you can cover her?

TAYLOR'S GUY #2
Why, where the hell are you going?

TAYLOR'S GUY #1
Man that Mexican we had before we got over here is goin right thru me. I gotta dump or I'm gonna wear it.

TAYLOR'S GUY #2
Alright hurry up, and make sure Rick doesn't catch you or your fuckin toast.

TAYLOR'S GUY #2
So, Taylor tells me you were some piece of ass for him and his buddies.

I'm one of his new buddies now, how bout you open wide like a tied up girl should.

ALICIA ROGERS
(smiling)
I'll tell you what. I'll do you one better.

TAYLOR'S GUY #2
Yeah? What's that?

TAYLOR'S GUY #1
Hey, what the hell's going on out there?

RICK TAYLOR
What the hell's going on down here. I leave you
two in charge...

TIME CUT
ALICIA ROGERS
Wake up asshole. You took my kid? Where is he?

RICK TAYLOR
Why the hell should I tell you?

ALICIA ROGERS
You're gonna tell me otherwise you're gonna lose
appendages one by one. See while you were out
cold, I went foraging thru your workbench for
implements of pain.

Now, one last time before I go medieval on you.
Where's my kid?

ALICIA ROGERS
O.K. mute, I know I can get you to say something,
might just be "Ahhhhhg" or some variation of
that, let's see.

RICK TAYLOR
(screaming)

Ahhhhhgh!

ALICIA ROGERS

Hey look at that, I was right!

Now dumbass, you got nine fingers, ten toes, your feeble manhood and not too much time left. I'll ask you again, where's my kid!

RICK TAYLOR
(hysterical)

You cut my goddamn finger off!

ALICIA ROGERS

I found a hatchet out there too, want me to cut your whole hand off? Where's my kid?

RICK TAYLOR

They've got him.

ALICIA ROGERS

Who is they?

RICK TAYLOR

Fox's security guys.

ALICIA ROGERS

Where are they keeping him?

RICK TAYLOR

I don't know.

                    RICK TAYLOR
                    (screaming)
Aaaaagh!
                  ALICIA ROGERS
That's for lying to me shithead. Where is he?

                    RICK TAYLOR
                     (labored)
A motel in Princeton, NJ near Fox's office.

                  ALICIA ROGERS
Which one?

                    RICK TAYLOR
                     (labored)
Chester Court...Chester Court

                  ALICIA ROGERS
How many are with him?

                    RICK TAYLOR
                     (fading)
Just one.

                  ALICIA ROGERS
                    (sweetly)
You know, I owe you one for giving up so easily.

                    RICK TAYLOR
You're gonna let me go?

                      ALICIA
Nah, changed my mind.
#

Title: "The Cacophony"

Source: "The Benefactor" *TV Script*

Genre: Drama

Tone: Light

Approx. Length: 2 Minutes

Character 1: Sandro **-** *Male, 40's*

Character 2: Chatty Kathy - *Female, 30's*

Character 3: The Benefactor **-** *Male, 50's*

Scene Description:
NYC Cab, present day.

EXT. NYC STREET CORNER - NIGHT

CHATTY KATHY
71st and Park

THE BENEFACTOR
My god woman, don't you ever take a breath or let
the other person get a word in edgewise?

CHATTY KATHY
(to the driver)
What did you just say?

SANDRO
Me? I didn't say anything.

CHATTY KATHY
Yes you did, I heard you.

THE BENEFACTOR
No, it was me.

Sandro, in order to preserve my sanity, please deposit this never ending cacophony at the next corner, with as much haste as you can muster.

CHATTY KATHY
(looking around)
I beg your pardon, I'm paying for this taxi, now take me to 71st and Park.

THE BENEFACTOR
Not anymore. Now please exit the vehicle and refrain from slamming the door.

CHATTY KATHY
I'm calling 311 to report you!

THE BENEFACTOR
Would you like me to place the call for you madam?
#

Title: "Scrubs"

Source: "The Benefactor" *TV Script*

Genre: Drama

Tone: Light

Approx. Length: 2 Minutes

Character 1: Sandro - *Male, 40's*

Character 2: Scrubs - *Male, 20's*

Character 3: The Benefactor - *Male, 50's*

Scene Description:
NYC Cab, present day.

SCRUBS

Good evening sir, Penn Station please.

SANDRO

My pleasure. Do you mind if I ask you a few questions?

SCRUBS

Sure, I just pulled an eighteen hour shift, and I don't know how sharp I'll be, so fire away.

SANDRO

What kind of doc are you?

SCRUBS

I'm a Pediatric Oncology resident.

SANDRO

I bet you have a ton of school loans to pay off.

SCRUBS
Six hundred thousand including interest. It crushes
me to think about it.

SANDRO
If you were to hit the lottery, would you still
practice medicine?

SCRUBS
Absolutely. I got into this because my cousin died
from inoperable brain cancer when he was ten.
I've dedicated my life to caring for these kids.

THE BENEFACTOR
Congratulations!

SCRUBS
Who's that?

SANDRO
(points up)
Listen.

THE BENEFACTOR
I am moved by your dedication, conviction and the
tireless work you do for those less fortunate.

Sandro, please present this young man with an
"A" envelope if you will.

Dear doctor, once you have found your seat on
the train, you may open the envelope. Then you
must follow the instructions inside. All that we ask
is that you make yourself available in the event we
require your services in the future. Is that clear?

SCRUBS
Uh, not really. What is this all about?

THE BENEFACTOR
It means that the elephant sitting on your chest wearing the college debt t-shirt has just picked his fat ass up and walked away. And, I must also add that your days and nights of salt-laden ramen are officially over.

I see that we have arrived at your destination. And with that my good man, I bid you a good night, sound sleep and continued success in your calling.

SCRUBS
I'm seriously confused, what's happening here?

THE BENEFACTOR
Follow the directions my son and all will be revealed.
#

Title: "The Suit"

Source: "The Benefactor" *TV Script*

Genre: Drama

Tone: Light

Approx. Length: 3 Minutes

Character 1: Sandro **-** *Male, 40's*

Character 2: Business Man - *Male, 30's*

Character 3: The Benefactor **-** *Male, 50's*

Scene Description:
NYC Cab, present day.

                    THE BENEFACTOR
Suit on your one o'clock.

                    SANDRO
Got 'em.

                    SUIT
395 South End Avenue

                    SANDRO
How are you tonight sir?

                    SUIT
Listen, no chit chat OK? Focus on the road and
get me home safely. That's your prime focus right
now. Got it?

                    SANDRO
Oh brother...

THE BENEFACTOR
OK Sparky. Here's how I see it.

A - Your tie is too tight and the blood flow to that rice krispie sized brain of yours has diminished your ability to act like a human friggin being.

B - You subscribe to the caste system and everyone below your seemingly vaunted station in life is less than pond scum to you.

C - You're just an arrogant prick who grew up surrounded by as many material substitutes for love that your emotionally vacant mommy and daddy could buy.

Or D - All of the above. That's my guess.

SUIT
(to Sandro)
Who is that, your dispatcher? You can't talk to me like that.

THE BENEFACTOR
I just did. What's the matter, never had someone put you in your place? I guess you're also the type who blamed the nanny on everything you broke? Now apologize to Sandro.

SUIT
Apologize for what?

THE BENEFACTOR
Sandro?

                    SANDRO
Yes sir?

                THE BENEFACTOR
Curb.

                    SANDRO
With pleasure.

                THE BENEFACTOR
Get out. Now!

                THE BENEFACTOR
I wish these idiots would stop slamming the door.
It hurts my ears and my feelings.

                    SANDRO
Maybe we should install a spring so that when
they slam the door, it shoots back at them and
knocks them on their ass.

                THE BENEFACTOR
I like the way you think Sandro.

Alright my good man, head south. Matter of fact,
let's play roulette and join the queue at World
Trade, maybe we'll get lucky.
#

Title: "The Offer"

Source: "The Benefactor" *TV Script*

Genre: Drama

Tone: Light

Approx. Length: 3 Minutes

Character 1: Roger - *Male, 40's*

Character 2: Scrubs - *Male, 20's*

Scene Description:
Law Office, present day.

ROGER
Hello Doctor Wainright.

SCRUBS
How do you know my name?

ROGER
That's inconsequential. Do you have your
envelope and letter?

SCRUBS
Yes, I do. Now what's this all about?

ROGER
Dr. Wainright, I must offer my congratulations and
ask you one simple question.

How would you like it?

SCRUBS
How would I like…?

I jump in a taxi after a hellaciously long day. I'm
tired and some voice comes over the taxi's sound
system telling me an elephant just got off my chest
and now you're asking me how I'd like it? Is this a
joke?

ROGER
It's not a joke Dr. Wainright. It's One Million
dollars. A gift from a very wealthy man who you
have clearly impressed.

SCRUBS
Are you kidding me? A Million dollars?

ROGER
The only thing I was kidding about was how you
wanted it. It's not like I could give you a laundry
sack full of tens, twenties and hundreds or have
you traipsing through Manhattan pushing a shop-
ping cart full of gold bullion around.

Not feasible. Would a cashier's check suffice?

Dr. Wainright, are you still with me?

SCRUBS
I think I'm in shock.

ROGER
Shall I call a doctor? Wait, you are a doctor.

SCRUBS
I'm…I'm OK. What do I have to do?

ROGER

You'll sign a lifetime non-disclosure document which states that you will never divulge in any verbal or printed form the nature of this interaction or any of the conversations that occurred in the taxi.

In other words Dr. Wainright, this never happened. Are we clear on that?

SCRUBS

Yes, I understand. One question though.

ROGER

What's that?

SCRUBS

What should I do with all this money. I've got a ton of school debt, but...

ROGER

I suggest you invest wisely Dr. Wainright.

I'm sorry to cut you short, but I must make a delivery to another lucky beneficiary. I wish you a good life Dr. Wainright.
#

Title: "Callie & Carissa"

Source: "The Benefactor" *TV Script*

Genre: Drama

Tone: Light

Approx. Length: 6 Minutes

Character 1: Sandro **-** *Male, 40's*

Character 2: Callie Vilgenza - *Female, 30's*

Character 3: Carissa Vilgenza **-** *Female, 16*

Character 4: The Benefactor **-** *Male, 50's*

Scene Description:
NYC Cab, present day.

SANDRO
Good evening, my name is Sandro. Where are you heading tonight?

CALLIE
Nice to meet you Sandro. This is my daughter Carissa and we need to go to Grand Central Terminal.

SANDRO
Were you here to see the museum?

CALLIE
Yes. I lost my husband on 9/11 and it took me this long to get up the courage to come down here.

SANDRO
Oh, I'm so sorry for both of you.

CALLIE

Thank you. He was a Pastry Chef at Windows on the World. He went in early that morning to prepare for a large lunch meeting and...

Well, this visit was for me as much as it was for my daughter. My husband never had a chance to meet her, she was born six months after we lost him.

SANDRO

How have the two of you been coping?

CALLIE

I don't come from a large family, so there's little support. His insurance covered a little, otherwise we do the best we can and take it one day at a time. Right sweetie?

CARISSA
(a little sad)

Yeah...

CALLIE

Are you OK cutie?

CARISSA

I'm OK. I feel really bad for all of those families.

SANDRO

Are you with me sir?

THE BENEFACTOR
Yes Sandro, I'm here.

Miss, can I ask your name?

CALLIE
Sandro, who is that?

SANDRO
It's O.K., Listen to what he has to say.

CALLIE
(hesitant)
My name is Callie Vilgenza

THE BENEFACTOR (V.O.)
Mrs. Vilgenza and Carissa, It is a pleasure to be with you tonight.

Although I consider myself a stoic person, your story has moved me greatly.

First off, please give Sandro your home address as he will be driving you and your daughter home tonight.

CALLIE
Oh no, that's OK. I wouldn't want to put you out.

THE BENEFACTOR
I insist, and I won't take no for an answer.

CALLIE
OK Sandro, the address is 488 Halstead Avenue in Harrison, NY

SANDRO

Thank you.

THE BENEFACTOR

Would you like Sandro to stop and pick up anything for you? Snacks or soda?

CARISSA

Can I get a soda mom?

CALLIE

Sure sweetie.

SANDRO

One soda coming up.

THE BENEFACTOR

Now Mrs. Vilgenza.

CALLIE

Please call me Callie.

THE BENEFACTOR

Callie, I'm breaking with tradition here, but what I'm about to tell you may make you and Carissa's life just a little bit better.

CALLIE

What do you mean?

THE BENEFACTOR

I was extremely lucky and very successful and I attribute it purely to the good fortune and great people I've met along the way.

I'm no longer able to enjoy the spoils of my success, so I've decided to help others who truly deserve my support.

Callie, have you and Carissa been able to get away at all over the past few years?

> CALLIE
> No, this trip was the only thing we've been able to do.

> THE BENEFACTOR (V.O.)
> Sandro, please present Callie and Carissa with an "A" and "B" envelope please.

Now, as I said, I'm breaking with tradition tonight. So my associate will travel to your home and present my offer.

> CALLIE
> What are you talking about? You're already driving us home. That's more than I expected.

> THE BENEFACTOR
> I can't go into details, but it's safe to say that my offer is worth much more than a one way trip to Westchester.

Now when my associate presents himself at your home, you are to give him both envelopes unopened and he will exchange them for my gift to you and your daughter. Is that clear?

> CALLIE
> Yes, but this is so unusual. Should I be concerned?

THE BENEFACTOR
Your only concern should be taking care of your family. I believe my gesture can help with that.

Ladies, I must ask your forgiveness as I must attend to a pressing matter here. It has been a pleasure and I wish you all the best.

Sandro, please contact me when you have dropped in Harrison, I have an idea I want to run up the flagpole.

SANDRO
Check.

CALLIE
Sandro, thank you so much for the ride. I'm sorry to ask this again but, is there anything I should worry about?

SANDRO
Not at all. One thing I must tell you is that you cannot disclose this to anyone. Carissa this goes for you as well.

CALLIE
I wouldn't know what to say, I still don't understand what's going on.

SANDRO
It will all make sense when our associate stops by.

CARISSA
Thank you for the soda Sandro.

                    SANDRO
You're welcome Carissa. Now please take care of
Mommy, you promise?

                    CARISSA
I will, I promise.

                    SANDRO
Good night everybody.
#

Title: "Home Stress"

Source: "The Benefactor" *TV Script*

Genre: Drama

Tone: Tense

Approx. Length: 2 Minutes

Character 1: Husband - *Male, 40's*

Character 2: Wife - *Female, 40's*

Scene Description:
Suburban home, present day.

WIFE

Bout' time you woke up. I've been paying bills for the past half hour while you're over there sawing enough wood for a bonfire.

What time did you finally crawl in from work?

HUSBAND

Three thirty

WIFE

Did you get paid yesterday?

HUSBAND

Yeah.

WIFE

I hope it was more than six hundred
dollars, I got more than that in this friggin pile here.

Go check the mailbox and see if the newspaper came yet.

HUSBAND

The paper came, but there was this envelope in the mailbox.

WIFE

What is it?

HUSBAND

I don't know.

WIFE

Let me see. Where was this?

HUSBAND

In the mailbox. What is it junk mail?

WIFE

Yeah, looks like it.

WIFE

Here, throw it out.

HUSBAND

So, what's for breakfast?

WIFE

Bowl of cereal.

Now leave me alone, I gotta figure out how I'm gonna stretch the pittance you bring home and pay all these damm bills.
#

Title: "Benefactor's Gift"

Source: "The Benefactor" *TV Script*

Genre: Drama

Tone: Light

Approx. Length: 2 Minutes

Character 1: Roger - *Male, 40's*

Character 2: Callie - *Female, 40's*

Character 3: Carissa - *Female, 16*

Scene Description:
Suburban home, present day.

CALLIE

Can I help you?

ROGER

My name is Roger Celestino and I'm representing a gentleman you conversed with the other night.

CALLIE

Oh yes, please come in. Would you like some coffee?

ROGER

No thank you, I'm coffeed out. Is your daughter home as well?

CALLIE

Yes, she is. I'll get her. Carissa can you come down for a minute?

CARISSA
O.K. Mom, be right there.

ROGER
Can we sit somewhere? Dining room perhaps?

CALLIE
Yes, of course.

ROGER
Do you have your envelopes?

CALLIE
Yes, here you go

ROGER
OK, what I'm about to tell you will be shocking, but I can guarantee that it is 100% legitimate.

Not only have you received an "A" envelope, but you've also received a "B" envelope as well. And for that I must congratulate you both.

CARISSA
What is this Mom?

CALLIE
I don't know, but I'm shaking.

ROGER
Not to worry ladies. It's all good.

Receipt of an "A" envelope entitles you to a cashier's check in the amount of One Million Dollars.

CARISSA

Oh my god!

ROGER

Are you O.K. Mrs. Vilgenza?

ROGER

The "B" envelope entitles you to an all expense paid two week trip to Disney World with a VIP behind the scenes tour plus Five Thousand Dollars spending money. You'll also be chauffeur driven to the airport where you'll travel to and from Orlando on a private jet.

Mother and daughter hug and cry together.

ROGER

Congratulations ladies and enjoy your trip. I'll leave this here and let myself out.
#

Title: "Ozzie's Zoo"

Source: "Ozzie's Limo" *TV Script*

Genre: Dramedy

Tone: Light

Approx. Length: 6 Minutes

Character 1: Sam - *Female, 20's*

Character 2: Linda - *Female, 30's*

Character 3: Angelo - *Male, 60's*

Character 4: John Mark - *Male, 30's*

Character 5: Flip - *Male 30's*

Character 6: Mufaddal - *Male, 50's*

Character 7: Ozzie - *Male, 60's*

Character 8: John B. - *Male, 50's*

Scene Description:
Limo Office, present day.

SAM

Ange, whatcha got for me today?

ANGELO

For you my dear, a hot and spicy Italian sausage

SAM

Holding her thumb and index finger an inch apart.

More like a cold and crusty Jimmy Dean, from what I heard.

JOHN MARC
Oh! Sam shoots a three pointer from the top of the
arc and scores!

ANGELO
You know, If you weren't cute, I'd knock you on
your ass right where you stand.

SAM
(laughing)
Still living in Fantasyland old man?

Gimme my damn jobs unless you wanna ride
home in an ambulance tonight.

ANGELO
Fine, take this one, and don't forget to thank me.

SAM
See ya boys!

JOHN MARC
(walking out)
Ange, I'm going to the bathroom, hook me up
when I get back.

FLIP
Whoa. You take care of her cause you wanna
bang her or you're afraid she'll hurt you?

MUFADDAL
This is unacceptable. In my country women defer
to men. Is she paying you, that why she get good
jobs?

ANGELO
Mufaddal, what country are you in now?

MUFADDAL
America.

ANGELO
Money talks here, don't forget it. And from now on
your new name is Muff Daddy.

MUFADDAL
What is this Muff Daddy? In my country Mufaddal
is one who is preferred, revered.

ANGELO
Muff Daddy is a compliment.

FLIP
(laughing)
Come on Ange, enough already. Gimme my damn
work for the day.

ANGELO
Here Flip, you happy now? Call me when you're
clear in midtown.

MUFADDAL
What am I second class citizen? I was a highly
respected chemical engineer back home. Here in
land of plenty, I am third in line behind a fighting
woman and man who tells jokes?

Angelo begins singing.

*"Charlie says Love my Good and Plenty
Charlie says Really Rings my Bell...."*

MUFADDAL

You malign my good name, sing songs while making me wait for work. I won't stand for this.

If I didn't need money to start my own limo company, I would wish you all to hell.

ANGELO

Don't bother Muff, every day around you guys is hell for me.

LINDA

What is going on here? Are you running an insane asylum full of misfits?

Ozzie shrugs.

OZZIE

Well at least they're my misfits.

So nice to see you honey. Please come in and sit down, we really need to talk.

LINDA

You know, I go from a nice life in LA, to getting picked up by a driver who's more interested in eating a sandwich than carrying my luggage. Then I come here and drivers are arguing with dispatch.

What happened? Mom dies and everything goes in the toilet?

I don't need this crap. I want acting jobs, not a lifetime of stress babysitting over age children.

OZZIE

Miho please, I called you here because I really need your help. Ever since your mom died, I don't have the strength to do this alone.

LINDA

Then, why don't you just put it up for sale?

OZZIE

I have clients that go back thirty years with me, I couldn't dump them off to anybody. I have to keep it in the family.

OZZIE

What is it?

JOHN B

Ozzie, it's John B.

OZZIE

Come in John. What's up?

                            JOHN B
John B just got off the phone with Mr. De Marco.
He said Jerry backed up into his driveway, popped
the trunk and waited in the car for Mr.DeMarco to
come out.

                            OZZIE
And?

                            JOHN B
Mr. De Marco came out with his bags, put them
into the trunk, closed it and went around to get in
the car. He opened the door, realized he forgot
something, closed it and started walking back to
the house.

                            OZZIE
OK?

                            JOHN B
Then Jerry drove off with the luggage in the trunk.

                            LINDA
And left the client behind? See, this is what I
mean. I don't have patience for stupidity like this.
#

Title: "Ozzie Diner"

Source: "Ozzie's Limo" *TV Script*

Genre: Dramedy

Tone: Light

Approx. Length: 4 Minutes

Character 1: Linda **-** *Female, 30's*

Character 2: Ozzie - *Male, 60's*

Scene Description:
Diner, present day.

INT. DINER - LATE AFTERNOON

LINDA

I understand that it's too much for you to deal with now that your older and mom's no longer around.

But, I'm torn between my aspirations and the obligation to help you out.

OZZIE

Honestly, I feel bad that I brought you back here, but I have no one else that I can trust.

Your brother James couldn't do it. He's so dumb, he has to call 311 every morning just to tie his shoes.

Big shot Ozzie Jr., ever since he hit Powerball he's forgotten where he came from.

                    LINDA
Lucky me.

                    OZZIE
Linda, I won't throw you to the wolves, I'll be there
to help you. Once you get up to speed, I'll start
taking some time off

                    LINDA
First we have to set some ground rules.

                    OZZIE
OK, I'm listening.

                    LINDA
The lunatics have to stop running the asylum.
If I need to play the bad guy, I'll do it.

                    OZZIE
You're not going to fire anybody are you?

                    LINDA
We'll see Pop. No promises.

                    OZZIE
Anything else?

                    LINDA
Yeah, If I read one of these idiots the riot act, I
don't want them to come crying to you.

Set up a meeting for tomorrow morning, you start
it off and I'll take it from there.

OZZIE

Hey, you remember when the family used to come here every Sunday?

LINDA

How could I forget. James building his Jenga stack of french fries, pours ketchup all over it then pulls the bottom one out waiting for the fries to come crashing down all over the table.

Ozzie Jr. mashing his food together till it becomes unrecognizable, then spooning it into his mouth.

I'm surprised the manager never kicked us out of here.

OZZIE

With the amount of business we gave him, I think we put his kids through college.

ANGELO

Ozz, sorry to bother you.

OZZIE

It's OK, what's up?

ANGELO

Sam was just arrested for assaulting a client, plus we have to pick her car up in Irvington.

LINDA

Oh great.

OZZIE

Which client?

ANGELO

Some new guy. They were on a wait and return when she said cops and a TV crew showed up. She got out to take a look, next thing I hear is an Irvington cop telling me she's under arrest.

OZZIE

OK, Linda and I will go up to the police station.

LINDA

Hell no. She rots there overnight.

OZZIE

Have somebody go up there and bring the car back. We'll get her in the morning.

ANGELO

Check.

LINDA

Is she for real? Assaulting clients?

OZZIE

Sam's a good kid. Something must have set her off.

LINDA

A client though? She has a whole lotta explaining to do. Maybe I should just fire her ass.

OZZIE

You gonna finish your fries sweetie?

LINDA

I lost my appetite Pop, take what you want.
#

Title: "Angelo Rules"

Source: "Dante's Limo" *TV Script*

Genre: Comedy

Tone: Light

Approx. Length: 5 Minutes

Character 1: Angelo - *Male, 60's*

Character 2: Mufaddal - *Male, 50's*

Character 3: John Mark - *Male 30's*

Character 2: Flip - *Male, 30's*

Character 3: Phone/Freelancer - *Male 30's*

Scene Description:
Limo Office, present day.

ANGELO

Dante's Limo.

DRIVER

Angelo, I'm in Connecticut and a turkey just slammed into my windshield.

ANGELO

A frozen turkey?

DRIVER

No you dumb ass, a friggin' wild turkey.

ANGELO

Dumb ass huh, the only wild turkey you hit flows out of a liquor bottle. So start picking the feathers out of your teeth, get your ass back here and try not to kill anything else except yourself.

FLIP

Can you throw me some real jobs please? I've had nothing but cheap ass taxi runs the past few days.

ANGELO

Awww, boo hoo to you.

MUFADDAL

Same for me too. I want good jobs as well.

ANGELO

Listen, if you guys bombard me all at once, I won't be able to finish the friggin schedule. Now back off.

JOHN MARC

I'm going to the bathroom, don't forget to hook me up with some of those lovely ladies.

A freelance driver walks in, opening his wallet, peeling off a $20 BILL, handing it to Angelo.

FREELANCE DRIVER

Here you go bud, watcha got for me today?

ANGELO

Marriott Marquis to Princeton, NJ, call me later.

FREELANCE DRIVER

Thanks Angelo, you're the best. See ya fellas.

FLIP

Whoa. Some freelancer goes first, throws you a twenty and gets a run to Princeton? Is that what it takes?

MUFADDAL

I must tell you, this is highly unacceptable. In my country we do things honorably.

ANGELO

Mufaddal, what country are we in now?

MUFADDAL

America.

ANGELO

Right. In this country, money talks, so don't forget it. And from now on, your name is Muff Daddy.

MUFADDAL

Mufaddal means one who is preferred, revered. What is this Muff Daddy you call me?

ANGELO

Muff Daddy is a compliment. Means you are an expert box licker.

MUFADDAL

Box licker?

ANGELO

Yeah, you know axe wound connoisseur, tongue swordsman.

MUFADDAL

That is disgusting! You like that?

ANGELO

Oh yeah baby, The ladies love it.

                    FLIP
                  (sniffing)
What's that smell?

                   ANGELO
It's either my dinner or the fact that I'm going
commando tonight.

                    FLIP
Ah, jeez.

                  MUFADDAL
You're in the army?

                    FLIP
                  (laughing)
No, Muff. That means he's not wearing any
underwear.

                  MUFADDAL
What disgusting pigs.

                   ANGELO
Here Flip, you happy now?

                    FLIP
I hope this isn't the only job for the night.

                   ANGELO
Nah, there's more. Call me when you're clear.

MUFADDAL
(agitated)
What am I second class citizen? I was a highly
respected chemical engineer back home. Here in
the land of plenty, I am third in line behind a
freelancer who bribes and man who tells jokes?

ANGELO
(singing)
"Charlie says Love my Good and Plenty.
Charlie says Really Rings my Bell...."

MUFADDAL
(yelling over his singing)
You malign my good name, sing songs while
making me wait for work. I won't stand for this. If I
didn't need money to start my own limo company,
I would wish you all to hell.

ANGELO
Don't bother Muff, every day around you friggin
guys is hell.

MUFADDAL
(yelling)
Penn Station to Waldorf? Because I'm Paki, you
give me Yellow Taxi jobs? Give me better or I quit
right now!
ANGELO
(smiling)
Lighten up there Muff, I got another one for you
after that. JFK to Midtown with a wait, then as di-
rected.

MUFADDAL
That is more like it. #

Title: "Flip's Act"

Source: "Dante's Limo" *TV Script*

Genre: Comedy

Tone: Light

Approx. Length: 3 Minutes

Character 1: Flip **-** *Male, 30's*

Character 2: Client - *Male, 40's*

Scene Description:
Moving Limo, present day.

FLIP
Good evening sir. How ya doin' tonight? My name is Flip.

CLIENT
Nice to meet you Flip. You know where we're headed?

FLIP
Yes sir, the Chelsea Savoy on 23rd.

CLIENT
That's it. Been driving a long time?

FLIP
Too long. But it pays the bills while I develop my stand up career.

CLIENT
Oh, so you're a comic.

                    FLIP
I'd like to think so.

                    CLIENT
Hit me with your best stuff.

                    FLIP
Alright. What did the green grape say to the purple
grape?

                    CLIENT
I don't know.

                    FLIP
Breathe you stupid bastard breathe.

                    CLIENT
Who told you that, a five year old?

                    FLIP
O.K. What time does an Asian go to the dentist?

                    CLIENT
Tell me.

                    FLIP
Tooth Hurty

                    CLIENT
These jokes suck.

                    FLIP
Alright then. What's the opposite of Christopher
Reeve?

                    CLIENT
Uh jeeze.

                    FLIP
Christopher Walken. What brand of suppositories
do Italians use?

                    CLIENT
No idea.

                    FLIP
Innuendo. Why do Jewish women like it from
behind?

                    CLIENT
Tell me.

                    FLIP
Because they hate to see anyone else have a
good time.

                    CLIENT
If that's your stage act, you got a long way to go.
Plus, you better lose those kid jokes unless you
wanna play backyard birthday parties the rest of
your life.

                    FLIP
Nah, I got a lot of other stuff I'm workin' on.

                    CLIENT
I hope so for your sake.
#

Title: "Stanley Starts"

Source: "Dante's Limo" *TV Script*

Genre: Comedy

Tone: Light

Approx. Length: 3 Minutes

Character 1: Angelo **-** *Male, 60's*

Character 2: Stanley - *Male, 50's*

Scene Description:
Limo Office, present day.

                    ANGELO
Stan, come here.

                    STANLEY
                    (angry)
It's Stanley. Don't ever call me Stan.

                    ANGELO
Relax there Stanley, don't ever call me Stan. I
wouldn't want you bustin' a blood vessel. Start
with this and I'll e-mail you the rest.

                    STANLEY
Bu...bu...But I don't have e-mail.

                    ANGELO
You need to get a smartphone and e-mail address
Stanley. Otherwise you're making extra work for
me. You have a pen and something to write on?

                    STANLEY
Yeah, that I have.

                    ANGELO
Terrific, we're makin' progress.

                    STANLEY
                    (reading)
Ek..ek..Excuse me, I can't do this job you gave
me.

                    DRIVER
Base come in.

                    ANGELO
Stand by..
                    (to Stanley)
What do you mean you can't do it?

                    STANLEY
I, I don't know New York City that well.

                    ANGELO
You don't know the city....Don't you have a GPS?

                    STANLEY
No, technology frightens me.

                    ANGELO
Oh brother...Paper maps?

                    STANLEY
No.

                    ANGELO
A compass?

                          STANLEY
No.

                          ANGELO
A sextant?

                          STANLEY
I..I don't have much experience with women.

                          ANGELO
No surprise there. How 'bout a globe?

                          STANLEY
I...I...I have one at home but it won't fit on the
dashboard.
                          (excited)
But...uh, I know the airports. I've taken friends
there a couple of times.

                          ANGELO
Fantastic.

                          STANLEY
Huh?

Angelo changes driver assignments on the
Schedule and hands a new job to Stanley.

                          ANGELO
Here, take this job and call me when you drop.

                          STANLEY
Wh...wh...Wait, I have to pick someone up at the
airport?

ANGELO

That's a problem too?

STANLEY

Uh yeah, I...I.. don't have any money for parking. I can do drop offs though.

ANGELO

Jeez Louise...you're no good to me if you're not prepared. Go have a seat, and I'll let you know if a simple job comes in.
#

Title: "Stanley's First, Part One"

Source: "Dante's Limo" *TV Script*

Genre: Comedy

Tone: Light

Approx. Length: 2 Minutes

Character 1: Angelo - *Male, 60's*

Character 2: Stanley - *Male, 50's*

Scene Description:
Limo Office, present day.

ANGELO
(yelling)

Stanley!! Front and center.

STANLEY

Did you call me?

ANGELO

I just got the perfect job for you.

STANLEY

Uh...Uh, what is it.

ANGELO

Here, take this. Now listen, you're gonna meet a client who has a rental car and boxes she needs you to deliver after you drop her off at the rental lot.

STANLEY

Wh...Wh..What's in the boxes, are they heavy?

ANGELO

How the hell would I know?

Listen, meet her at the office, follow her to the rental lot, take her to the terminal, then drop the boxes off where she tells you. It's that simple.

STANLEY

Uh, I guess so.

So, C...C...Can you map it out for me?

ANGELO

Stanley, did you remember to put your big boy pants on this morning?

STANLEY

Huh?

ANGELO

I'll print this one out, but you gotta buy a GPS, cause I don't have the time or patience to spoon feed you.

STANLEY

Where can I get one?

ANGELO

Smash the window of the next car you see and take theirs.

STANLEY
(incredulous)

I...I can't do that!

ANGELO

Well, how 'bout an electronics store. You think
they might sell 'em?

STANLEY

Gee, I guess.

ANGELO

Well there you go. Here's the map, now get going.
Call me if you have any problems.
#

Title: "Stanley's First, Part Two"

Source: "Dante's Limo" *TV Script*

Genre: Comedy

Tone: Light

Approx. Length: 4 Minutes

Character 1: Angelo - *Male, 60's*

Character 2: Stanley - *Male, 50's*

Character 3: Client - *Female 30's*

Scene Description:
Office Park & Rental Facility, present day.

STANLEY

Stanley to base.

ANGELO

Go ahead.

STANLEY

I'm on location, but I don't see a rental car…

You…You scared the life out of me!

CLIENT

You ready to go? I can't miss this flight.

STANLEY

Uh…uh where's your rental car?

CLIENT

Over there, just follow me when I pull up. Here's the address where you have to drop the boxes. Pop the trunk so I can put them in.

                    STANLEY

Stanley to base, I found the client.

                    ANGELO
Hallelujah.

TIME CUT

EXT. RENTAL LOT - EVENING

                    CLIENT
Sorry it took so long, please rush me over to the
main terminal, I'll probably just make it.

                    STANLEY
No problem sir.

*Stanley throws it into reverse, running over the
spikes blowing all four tires*

                    CLIENT
What the hell was that??

                    STANLEY
Uh...Uh...I don't know.

CLIENT
(pissed)
Ah, for Christ sakes, you blew all four tires you friggin' idiot! Now I'm gonna miss my flight!

Son of a bitch!

What's your name?

STANLEY
S...s...s...Stanley

CLIENT
Well s...s...Stanley, that has to be the most asinine thing I have ever seen in my years of traveling. Nice going you dumb shit! So help me god, those boxes better be delivered tonight or there will be hell to pay.

STANLEY
S...s...Stanley to base.

ANGELO
Go ahead.

STANLEY
Uh...uh, I've got uh flat tires.

ANGELO
Did you say tires with an "s"?

STANLEY
Yes.

ANGELO
How many?

                    STANLEY
Four.

                    ANGELO
Are you kidding me? How the hell did you do that
Stanley?

Was the client in the car with you?

                    STANLEY
Yes, but she...she left. I still have to deliver the
b...b..boxes, so I need four n...n...new tires right
away.

                    ANGELO
You need your head examined Stanley. Ask the
rental guys if they can help you while I figure
something out.

By the way Stanley,

                    STANLEY
Yes?

                    ANGELO
Impeccable start to your first day.
#

Title: "John Mark – Male Prostitute"

Source: "Dante's Limo" *TV Script*

Genre: Comedy

Tone: Light

Approx. Length: 2 Minutes

Character 1: John Mark **-** *Male, 30's*

Character 2: Woman - *Female, 50's*

Character 3: Husband - *Male 50's*

Scene Description:
High Rise Condo, present day.

WOMAN

I must say, you're a fine specimen for your race. Get over here so I can unwrap that tasty bar of chocolate you brought me.

JOHN MARC

I promise, you won't be disappointed.

TIME CUT

WOMAN

Oh yes, do me you strapping Mandingo Warrior.

A nebbish man clumsily falls through closet doors holding a video camera.

WOMAN

Jesus H. Christ Marvin, what the hell is your problem?

JOHN MARC
Whoa, who the hell is he?

WOMAN
Don't worry sweetie. That's just my clumsy limp
dick husband.

HUSBAND
(on the floor)
I tripped over your goddamn shoe collection
Imelda and lost my balance. O.K.?

WOMAN
Now who's gonna fix my closet doors Marvin? You
sure as hell can't. Somebody asks to borrow your
screwdriver, you go scampering off for the vodka.

JOHN MARC
You people are miles past insane.

WOMAN
(sweetly)
Maybe so stud, but you loved every minute of it.

WOMAN
(angrily, to Husband)
I sure hope you got all that on tape Marvin.

HUSBAND
Nobody uses tape anymore you old hag.
#

Title: "G-Ro Realty"

Source: "Dante's Limo" *TV Script*

Genre: Comedy

Tone: Light

Approx. Length: 1 Minute

Character 1: Gino **-** *Male, 30's*

Character 2: Rosalie - *Female, 30's*

Scene Description:
Residential Area, present day.

Gino is wearing a long leather jacket over his guinea t-shirt and standing in front of a house with Rosalie by his side.

GINO

Hey, you in the market for a house or apartment on a strictly short term basis?

My girl Rosalie here hooked us up big time. See Rosalie works in real estate.

ROSALIE

I ansa da phones.

GINO

Nah, she does more than that, she's got her ear to the ground.

Rosalie drops down and puts her ear to the ground.

                    GINO
                  (pissed)
Get off the ground Ro, we're on TV.

We got furnished houses.

*He opens his left breast side jacket to reveal lines
of house keys. Rosalie points to them like a
model.*

And we got unfurnished houses.

*Opens right side breast jacket revealing more
keys, Rosalie points again.*

Folks, this is a limited time offer, so call now.
1 800 WON'T LAST that's 1 800 WON'T LAST for
an amazing once in a lifetime deal.

Say good bye Ro

                  ROSALIE
                  (waving)
Good bye Ro.
#

Title: "G-Ro Demolition"

Source: "Dante's Limo" *TV Script*

Genre: Comedy

Tone: Light

Approx. Length: 1 Minute

Character 1: Gino - *Male, 30's*

Scene Description:
Residential Area, present day.

Gino is dressed in contractor clothes a hard hat and wearing a tool belt.

GINO

This is not a drill!

Gino holds up a Sledgehammer.

It's a Sledgehammer.

Hi Friends,did you just find out that the bank just foreclosed on your house and you're pissed that they're gonna sell it to some schmuck for pennies on the dollar?

If you agree that nobody should get what's rightfully yours, call me. My friends and I would be more than happy to turn your place into a pile of rubble and dust. Tell your bank FU and give me a call right now. 1800 Demo that's 1800 Demo. Call in the next ten minutes and I'll make sure Rocco gets a piece of the action.
#

Title: "G-Ro Investigations"

Source: "Dante's Limo" *TV Script*

Genre: Comedy

Tone: Light

Approx. Length: 1 Minute

Character 1: Gino **-** *Male, 30's*

Character 2: Rosalie - *Female, 30's*

Scene Description:
Office, present day.

Gino and Rosalie are dressed in suits and fedoras sitting behind a desk in a darkened office.

ROSALIE
Is your significant other doin the horizontal nasty with someone other than you?

GINO
You wanna prove that somebody's dirty, but you just don't know how?

RO & GINO
Welcome to G-Ro Investigations

ROSALIE
Private dicks if you will.

GINO
We'll set loose our network of trusted associates to get you what you need.

ROSALIE

You want photos, video? If ya want a Polaroid we
can get that too. Can we?

GINO

I guess so.

ROSALIE

No matta what you want found out, we'll found it
for ya.

GINO

G-Ro Investigations

ROSALIE & GINO

*Gino is holding up a magnifying glass and Rosalie,
paper maps.*

GINO

We got the tools…

ROSALIE

…as long as you got the money.

2nd floor just above McNulty's bar. Knock four
times so we know it's you.

And G, don't forget yours is private. You even
think of taking that thing elsewhere, I'll get the
poultry scissors and cut that chicken right off.

Snip, snip

GINO

Hey!
#

Title: "G-Ro Home Improvement"

Source: "Dante's Limo" *TV Script*

Genre: Comedy

Tone: Light

Approx. Length: 1 Minute

Character 1: Gino - *Male, 30's*

Character 2: Rosalie - *Female, 30's*

Scene Description:
Residential Area, present day.

Gino and Rosalie are dressed in contractor clothes, hard hats and wearing tool belts.

GINO
Is your batchroom lookin like it was built back in the '60s?...The 1860's?

ROSALIE
Are reservations the only thing you make in your kitchen?

GINO
Isn't it time you brought that dump up to respectable standards?

ROSALIE
We're G-Ro Home Improvements.

GINO
Certified green baby!

Rosalie rubs her thumb and index fingers together

                    GINO
Our green certification comes from the fact that we
only use recycled materials on all of our projects.

                    ROSALIE
Recycled screws, nails, wood, fixtures...you name
it, we'll use it

                    GINO
Not only do we redo kitchens and batchrooms, we
also do home construction as well.

Stick built

Rosalie holds up two small wood sticks.

And modular.

*Rosalie holds a Lego piece in each hand and then
connects them, smiling.*

                    GINO
So get your best price for any home improvement
project and we'll beat it.

                    ROSALIE
Like a misbehaving red haired stepchild.

                    GINO
Ro!

                    ROSALIE
Sorry G, it slipped out.

Rosalie fakes a hand covering her mouth.

                    GINO
You know it makes me hot for you when you talk
like that, but save the drunken sailor act for off
camera, k?

                  ROSALIE
               (thumbs up)
Got it G.

                    GINO
So whatever you need, call G-Ro Home
Improvement, your local do it all for the green
contractor.

                  ROSALIE
Are we done here G? I'm late for my mani/pedi.

                    GINO
Yeah, we're done.

As Rosalie steps away, Gino slaps her butt.

                  ROSALIE
Gino!
#

Title: "G-Ro Cleaning"

Source: "Dante's Limo" *TV Script*

Genre: Comedy

Tone: Light

Approx. Length: 1 Minute

Character 1: Gino **-** *Male, 30's*

Character 2: Rosalie - *Female, 30's*

Scene Description:
Residential Area, present day.

Gino and Rosalie are dressed in aprons and holding a mop and duster.

GINO

Is your house a freakin mess?

ROSALIE

Are you a shoe in for that psycho hoarders show?

GINO

If that's you, good luck pigpen. We specialize in the pricier parts of town

ROSALIE & GINO

We're G-Ro Cleaning

ROSALIE

You name it, we'll clean you out.

                          GINO
Got junk to cart away? Leave it to us...I mean,
leave us the keys and disappear for a coupla
hours, and when you come back...

                        ROSALIE
Boy, will you be surprised.

                          GINO
Have you had bad experiences with other low
class cleaning services that don't move stuff and
clean around 'em?

                        ROSALIE
Don't worry, we'll move 'em for ya.

                          GINO
Got high end electronics? We'll move them too.

                        ROSALIE
Cha Ching!

                          GINO
So, from knick knacks in your den to cars in your
garage, Call G-Ro Cleaning today for our One
Stop Cleanout Special.

                        ROSALIE
Knick knack paddy whack give this girl a bone!

                          GINO
                       (Dice Clay)
Oh!
#

Title: "G-Ro We Drive"

Source: "Dante's Limo" *TV Script*

Genre: Comedy

Tone: Light

Approx. Length: 1 Minute

Character 1: Gino **-** *Male, 30's*

Character 2: Rosalie - *Female, 30's*

Scene Description:
Office, present day.

Gino and Rosalie are dressed in dark suits, white shirts and black ties wearing chauffeur's hats sitting behind a desk in an office.

GINO
Are you heading to the airport and gonna drive there yourself?

ROSALIE
The freakin' traffic, the bozos that drive like crap and the parking. Oofa!

GINO
Or you planning to have a taxi or limo take you there?

ROSALIE
(dialect)

Rosalie holds up a G-Ro We Drive waiting sign with "Hey You" written on it.

Hello my friend! My name is Akbar.

                         GINO
Ro!

                        ROSALIE
                     (waves him off)
Ah, frig 'em.

                         GINO
Welcome to G-Ro We Drive!

                        ROSALIE
One call and one of our super experienced drivers
will drive you there...

                         GINO
                      (pointing)
In your own car!

                        ROSALIE
And, if you're real nice, throw him a fat tip and the
resale value of your car is up there, he may even
wash it and get the oil changed for ya.

                         GINO
And when you get back...

                        ROSALIE
                     (interrupts)
Call now 1 800 WE DRIVE, that's 1800 WE
DRIVE.

                         GINO
And leave your car with us!
#

Title: "G-Ro Rooter"

Source: "Dante's Limo" *TV Script*

Genre: Comedy

Tone: Light

Approx. Length: 1 Minute

Character 1: Gino - *Male, 30's*

Character 2: Rosalie - *Female, 30's*

Scene Description:
Residential Area, present day.

Gino and Rosalie are dressed in overalls. Gino holds a pipe wrench and Rosalie a plunger.

ROSALIE
Do you need your pipes cleaned?

GINO

Boy, do I!

ROSALIE
Stick a sock in it, you got some last week.

GINO
Drains runnin slow cause ya got a bunch of long haired females cloggin 'em up?

ROSALIE
Or ya got guys takin godzilla sized dumps after a rough night of less than stellar surf & turf?

GINO
Got kids throwin stuff in the terlit that don't belong
there?

ROSALIE
There's no R in toilet you putz!

GINO
No matter what keeps your tub, toilet or sink from
doin the old counter clockwise swirl...

ROSALIE
Our crack staff of highly trained technicians can
fish it out or push it through. Whatever it takes...

GINO
To get that human lemonade and toilet fish on its
way to that stinky place on the west side.

ROSALIE
Why'd they put a basketball court on top of a
sewage plant anyway?

GINO
Beats me. G-Ro Rooter at your service 24 hours
a day, 7 days a week, 364 days a year.

ROSALIE
Why not 365?

GINO
We're closed on your birthday remember?

ROSALIE
Oh yeah, that's right.

                    GINO
G-Ro Rooter 1800 WE SUCK, that's
1800 WE SUCK.

                    ROSALIE
            (pointing the plunger)
Call now!

    #

Title: "1-800-GET LOST"

Source: "Dante's Limo" *TV Script*

Genre: Comedy

Tone: Light

Approx. Length: 1 Minute

Character 1: Gino - *Male, 30's*

Character 2: Gino's Ma - *Female, 60's*

Scene Description:
Residential Area, present day.

> GINO

Hey, you in the market to disappear? Need to skip out on a debt or as the kids say, get off the grid?

I got safe houses up the wazoo, places they'll never find you. I could even drop you in Jersey.

I get lost in Jersey.

A mumu wearing, curlers in the hair mother sticks her head out of the screen door and yells to Gino.

> MOM
> (yelling)

Gino, phone!

> *GINO*

Who is it Ma?

> MOM

How the hell should I know.

                    GINO
Well, could you ask?

                    MOM
What am I your secretary or something?

                    GINO
Please Ma?

Anyway, pack a bag, bring me a healthy stack of
dead presidents and consider yourself gone.

Don't wait till it's too late, call 1 800 GET LOST,
that's 1 800 GET LOST.

Mom sticks her head out again.

                    MOM
He says his name is Jimmy.

                    GINO
Jimmy the Fish or Jimmy Skates?

                    MOM
Listen buster, I ain't getting back on the phone for
you. Get your lazy ass in here and figure it out
yourself.
                    GINO
                  (frustrated)
Ah, for crying out loud.
#

Title: "1-800-FOOD FOR FUN"

Source: "Dante's Limo" *TV Script*

Genre: Comedy

Tone: Light

Approx. Length: 1 Minute

Character 1: Rosalie - Female, 30's

Scene Description:
Residential Area, present day

ROSALIE
Hey, you in the market for a little company
tonight?

Not me!

I got a bunch of girls that if you wine and dine 'em,
the dessert cart just might swing around for ya, if
you know what I mean.

And no Mickey D's, Popeye's or Subway. Got it?
Real food, like a knife and fork joint with candles
and a short Italian guy playin violin.

And if you're pullin up blastin rap music in some
hooptie that sounds like a leaf blower on steroids,
keep goin. You gotta be showin up in a BMW,
Mercedes or a Lexus. You drivin something better
than that, maybe I might be interested...

Gino stick his head out of the screen door.

GINO
Hey Ro, watcha doin?

ROSALIE
(yells over her shoulder)
I got my own thing goin on.

So gimme a call, 1 800 FOOD 4 FUN that's
1 800 FOOD 4 FUN. And don't be a loser, K?
#

Title: "Momma's Fromage"

Source: "Dante's Limo" *TV Script*

Genre: Comedy

Tone: Light

Approx. Length: 1 Minute

Character 1: Gino **-** *Male, 30's*

Character 2: Rosalie - *Female, 30's*

Scene Description:
Supermarket Cheese Counter, present day

Gino and Rosalie are dressed in berets and mustaches behind the counter of a cheese shop.

GINO
Hey!, Welcome to Mamma's Frommage!

ROSALIE
That's French for Mama's Cheese.

GINO
Everybody loves Mama.

ROSALIE
(deadpan)
They never met my mother.

GINO
That's true...but everybody loves cheese right?

ROSALIE
I guess...

GINO

At Momma's Frommage, we carry the best
domestic cheese in cans, blocks and individually
wrapped slices.

And we also carry that goofy nutball cheese.

ROSALIE

Ha, that's funny. Nutball, get it?

GINO
(mispronounces)
And we got imported cheese too. Camembert,
Gorgonzola, Jarlsberg and Gouda. Guess that's
short for good enough, huh?

ROSALIE

This one smells like your friggin sneakers, and this
one says made in Jersey.

GINO

Ro, if it comes over the river, it's imported.

ROSALIE

Hey, we got any Toe Cheese? And what the hell is
Head Cheese anyway?

GINO

Ro, get serious. We're on TV.

ROSALIE

Oui, Oui

GINO

That means yes in French.

ROSALIE

No, that means I gotta go tinkle.

GINO

Great. Come on down to Mama's Frommage. Find us at the end of Fifth between the peep show and the rub and tug joint.

ROSALIE
(misprounouncing)

Over Wa!
#

Title: "Chico's Bedding"

Source: "Dante's Limo" *TV Script*

Genre: Comedy

Tone: Light

Approx. Length: 1 Minute

Character 1: Chico - *Male, 40's*

Character 2: Customer - *Male, 30's*

Scene Description:
Used Bedding Store, present day

                    CHICO
Are you in the market for a mattress, but don't
wanna pay extra for two goons to come traipsing
through your boudoir?

I don't think so.

Come on down to Chico's Slightly Used Bedding
Emporium. We offer the best in take it yourself
mattresses and boxsprings. And all of our
mattresses are factory sealed right on the
premises.

With every purchase of a closely matching
boxspring and mattress, we'll throw in enough
rope at no extra charge, so that your new used
bed won't go airborne on you.

So come on down to Chico's Slightly Used
Bedding Emporium 456 Bruckner Boulevard
in the Bronx right across from Mr. Softee.

Call 1-800-323-STAIN that's 1-800-323-STAIN.

CUSTOMER
Hey Chico, this mattress really stinks.

CHICO
Bet the price didn't stink huh? Drive around for a coupla hours, it'll air out.
#

Title: "M.E.A.T"

Source: "Dante's Limo" *TV Script*

Genre: Comedy

Tone: Light

Approx. Length: 1 Minute

Character 1: Omar **-** *Male, 20's*

Character 2: Deuce - *Male, 20's*

Character 3: Mabel - *Female, 70's*

Scene Description:
City street, present day

                    OMAR
Yo, yo, yo. Proud to say we're open for business.

                    MABEL
Who's we?

                    OMAR
You can call us Meat!

                    DEUCE
Mobile Electronics and 'Tainment.

                    OMAR
Check it out, we got microwaves.

                    DEUCE
Ding! Comes complete with your first meal!

                    OMAR
We got vacuums too!

DEUCE
They really suck!

OMAR
Car Stereos, Jewelry, Silverware, you name it.

DEUCE
We also take special orders.

OMAR
No matter what you want, our prices are the lowest in town!

OMAR AND DEUCE
Cause nobody beats our meat!

They high five each other.

MABEL
You boys know what you can get me?

OMAR
Name it.

MABEL
Yuban.

DEUCE
What's that?

MABEL
Yuban get your ass off my street, before I call the cops.

OMAR
Damm woman, that's cold.
#

Testaforte Entertainment develops Feature Film and Television scripts in addition to publishing Print on Demand titles. These projects include:

The Driver – *Drama Short*

A limo driver in a modified Town Car picks up unsuspecting people bound for their final destination.

Exacting Retribution – *Revenge Thriller*

A young boy survives the murder of his family and the murder of his stepfather. He channels that anger into a successful revenge for hire business.

Justified Retribution – *Revenge Thriller*

A woman redeems herself through martial arts and building a successful law firm after she is sexually assaulted at a fraternity party. She then sets out exacting revenge on each of the men responsible.

The Benefactor – *Half Hour TV Drama*

A disabled billionaire, his wealth manager and a NYC Taxi Driver vet passengers to determine who's worthy of receiving life changing gifts.

Ozzie's Limo – *Half Hour TV Dramedy*

A reluctant LA based actress comes back east to help her aging father run his limo business. She quickly learns to deal with the bizarre characters and daily situations that confront her.

Dante's Limo – *Half Hour TV Comedy*

A caustic limo dispatcher spends his days managing drivers who consistently find themselves in comedically undesirable situations

Published titles available from
Testaforte Entertainment

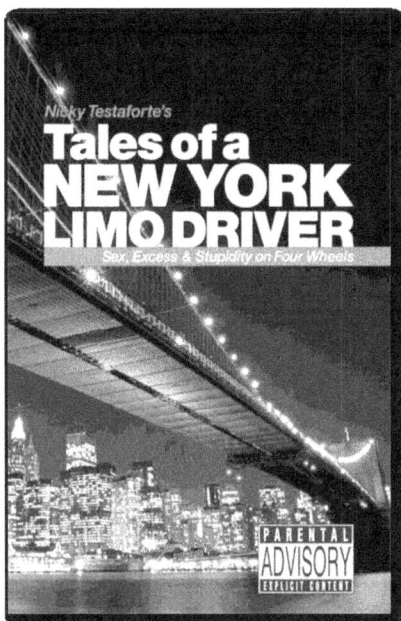

Available in Print and e-book from:

amazon   Smashwords   iBooks

And, coming soon as an Audiobook from:

iTunes   audible

Nicky Testaforte's

Exacting Retribution

Revenge Done Right

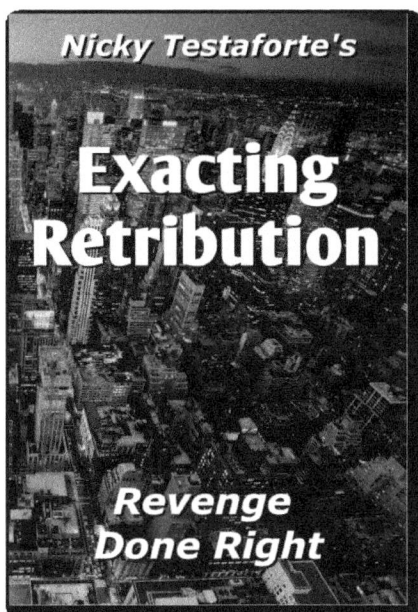

Available in Print and e-book from:

amazon   Smashwords™   iBooks

And coming soon as an Audiobook from:

iTunes   audible

Nicky Testaforte's

Justified Retribution

**Hell Hath
No Fury...**

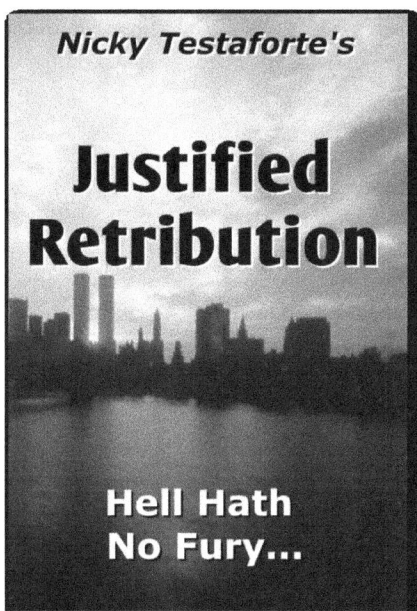

Available in Print and e-book from:

amazon   Smashwords   iBooks

And coming soon as an Audiobook from:

iTunes   audible

Nicky Testaforte's

Black Book

of
**50 Original
Dark Drama and
Comedy Scenes
For Actors**

Vol. 1

Available in print from

amazon

**Discounted bulk orders for
acting schools available through
Testaforte Entertainment
email: blackbookorders@gmail.com**

Testaforte
Entertainment
Feature Films Television Publishing

www.ingramcontent.com/pod-product-compliance
Lightning Source LLC
LaVergne TN
LVHW051049080426
835508LV00019B/1786